Automated Grammatical Error Detection for Language Learners

Second Edition

Synthesis Lectures on Human Language Technologies

Editor
Graeme Hirst, *University of Toronto*

Synthesis Lectures on Human Language Technologies is edited by Graeme Hirst of the University of Toronto. The series consists of 50- to 150-page monographs on topics relating to natural language processing, computational linguistics, information retrieval, and spoken language understanding. Emphasis is on important new techniques, on new applications, and on topics that combine two or more HLT subfields.

Automated Grammatical Error Detection for Language Learners, Second Edition
Claudia Leacock, Martin Chodorow, Michael Gamon, and Joel Tetreault
2014

Ontology-Based Interpretation of Natural Language
Philip Cimiano, Christina Unger, and John McCrae
2014

Web Corpus Construction
Roland Schäfer and Felix Bildhauer
2013

Recognizing Textual Entailment: Models and Applications
Ido Dagan, Dan Roth, Mark Sammons, and Fabio Massimo Zanzotto
2013

Linguistic Fundamentals for Natural Language Processing: 100 Essentials from Morphology and Syntax
Emily M. Bender
2013

Semi-Supervised Learning and Domain Adaptation in Natural Language Processing
Anders Søgaard
2013

Semantic Relations Between Nominals
Vivi Nastase, Preslav Nakov, Diarmuid Ó Séaghdha, and Stan Szpakowicz
2013

Computational Modeling of Narrative
Inderjeet Mani
2012

Natural Language Processing for Historical Texts
Michael Piotrowski
2012

Sentiment Analysis and Opinion Mining
Bing Liu
2012

Discourse Processing
Manfred Stede
2011

Bitext Alignment
Jörg Tiedemann
2011

Linguistic Structure Prediction
Noah A. Smith
2011

Learning to Rank for Information Retrieval and Natural Language Processing
Hang Li
2011

Computational Modeling of Human Language Acquisition
Afra Alishahi
2010

Introduction to Arabic Natural Language Processing
Nizar Y. Habash
2010

Cross-Language Information Retrieval
Jian-Yun Nie
2010

Automated Grammatical Error Detection for Language Learners
Claudia Leacock, Martin Chodorow, Michael Gamon, and Joel Tetreault
2010

Data-Intensive Text Processing with MapReduce
Jimmy Lin and Chris Dyer
2010

Automated Grammatical Error Detection for Language Learners, Second Edition

Claudia Leacock, Martin Chodorow, Michael Gamon, and Joel Tetreault

ISBN: 978-3-031-01025-5   paperback
ISBN: 978-3-031-02153-4   ebook

DOI 10.1007/978-3-031-02153-4

A Publication in the Springer series
SYNTHESIS LECTURES ON HUMAN LANGUAGE TECHNOLOGIES

Lecture #25
Series Editor: Graeme Hirst, *University of Toronto*
Series ISSN
Synthesis Lectures on Human Language Technologies
Print 1947-4040   Electronic 1947-4059

Automated Grammatical Error Detection for Language Learners

Second Edition

Claudia Leacock
CTB McGraw-Hill

Martin Chodorow
Hunter College and the Graduate Center, City University of New York

Michael Gamon
Microsoft Research

Joel Tetreault
Yahoo! Labs

SYNTHESIS LECTURES ON HUMAN LANGUAGE TECHNOLOGIES #25

ABSTRACT

It has been estimated that over a billion people are using or learning English as a second or foreign language, and the numbers are growing not only for English but for other languages as well. These language learners provide a burgeoning market for tools that help identify and correct learners' writing errors. Unfortunately, the errors targeted by typical commercial proofreading tools do not include those aspects of a second language that are hardest to learn.

This volume describes the types of constructions English language learners find most difficult—constructions containing prepositions, articles, and collocations. It provides an overview of the automated approaches that have been developed to identify and correct these and other classes of learner errors in a number of languages.

Error annotation and system evaluation are particularly important topics in grammatical error detection because there are no commonly accepted standards. Chapters in the book describe the options available to researchers, recommend best practices for reporting results, and present annotation and evaluation schemes.

The final chapters explore recent innovative work that opens new directions for research. It is the authors' hope that this volume will continue to contribute to the growing interest in grammatical error detection by encouraging researchers to take a closer look at the field and its many challenging problems.

KEYWORDS

grammatical error detection, statistical natural language processing, learner corpora, linguistic annotation

Martin Chodorow: To Mamie,
and to the memory of my parents.

Claudia Leacock: To my daughters,
Tess Elspeth Dougherty and Tracy Duva Dougherty.

Contents

Acknowledgments

We are grateful to Øistein E. Andersen, Aoife Cahill, Robert Dale, Michael Flor, Jennifer Foster, Ross Israel, John Lee, Nitin Madnani, Hwee Tou Ng, and an anonymous reviewer for their feedback and helpful suggestions.

Claudia Leacock, Martin Chodorow, Michael Gamon, and Joel Tetreault
January 2014

CHAPTER 1

Introduction

1.1 INTRODUCTION TO THE SECOND EDITION

Since the first edition of this volume was published in 2010, research in grammatical error detection and correction has moved from being presented primarily in small workshops to being presented in the main programs of major conferences. At the ACL conference in 2011, a main conference session was devoted entirely to grammatical error detection.

In the first edition, we painted a gloomy picture of the difficulties encountered in comparing the performance of different error detection and correction systems, using the word "impossible" more than once. Since 2010, the picture has notably changed. There have been three shared tasks where independent research teams used identical training materials, testing materials, and evaluation metrics.

This field has increased not only in prominence but also in the sheer volume of reported research. In the first edition, we were able to cover all of the published work in automated error detection and correction, but this is no longer possible. Instead, for the second edition, we have tried to focus more on the techniques that are reported in conference papers than on the details of specific studies.

The field of grammatical error detection and correction has grown up, and with that have come many exciting new developments. It is the purpose of this edition to include the many steps, large and small, that the field has taken.

1.2 NEW TO THE SECOND EDITION

The early chapters in this volume, "Background of Automated Grammatical Error Detection" and "Special Problems of Language Learners," have been updated, where appropriate, but they are not substantially different from the first edition. What used to be the chapter "Language Learner Data," an annotated compendium of learner corpora, has been moved into an Appendix. The new Chapter 4, "Evaluating Error Detection Systems," has been expanded to include evaluation metrics for the shared tasks and detailed guidelines for reporting results. The chapter on article and preposition errors has been wholly revised. The original chapter exhaustively covered all of the published research. This is no longer possible. The new chapter, "Data-Driven Approaches to Article and Preposition Errors," now teases apart and describes the technical approaches used by data-driven systems. The chapters on "Collocation Errors" and "Different Errors and Different Approaches" have also been updated. The latter has been expanded to include recent work on punctuation errors and on determining whether a sentence as a whole contains an error. "Annotating Learner Errors" now includes detailed coverage about using crowdsourcing and mining community-driven revision logs. Finally, the "Emerging Directions" chapter covers the Helping Our Own (HOO) shared tasks for 2011 and 2012 and CoNLL 2013 shared task, as well as machine translation techniques and real-time crowdsourcing for grammatical error correction.

1.3   WORKING DEFINITION OF *GRAMMATICAL ERROR*

Written *grammatical errors* are often categorized as being errors in either grammar, usage or mechanics—and sometimes include a subset of spelling errors. Fraser and Hodson [1978] defined the distinction between grammar and usage as follows:

> We must distinguish between grammar and usage. ...Each language has its own systematic ways through which words and sentences are assembled to convey meaning. This system is grammar. But within the general grammar of a language, certain alternative ways of speaking and writing acquire particular social status, and become the conventional usage habits of dialect groups.

Grammars contain specific rules about the syntax and morphology of a language. For example, a prepositional phrase can follow an intransitive verb but a noun phrase cannot. However, grammars generally do not handle questions of usage such as which preposition is the best choice in a given context, or whether the use of the definite or indefinite article or no article at all is more appropriate. These kinds of usage errors, we find, are the most frequent errors of language learners.

In written language, there are also mechanical errors that include obvious typographical mistakes such as *a the house* and some misuse of punctuation. The most frequent error in English is the misuse of commas, although not all of these errors are purely mechanical, given the complexity of comma-placement rules.

Finally, while spelling errors are not usually considered grammatical errors, some classes of spelling errors, we argue, are. Some language learners' spelling errors involve a violation of syntactic and/or morphological regularities, and should be covered under the umbrella of grammatical errors. For example, *he writed* contains a word that does not exist in English. Technically, it could be considered a spelling or even a typographical error, especially if a native speaker of English produced the text. However, as Heift and Schulze [2007] point out, language learners can produce misspellings based on either a misapplication of morphological rules or other influences from their native language (L1), or from their incomplete knowledge of the morphology and phonology of the language being learned (L2). In the example of a learner using *writed*, we can hypothesize that this form is influenced by an incomplete knowledge of English irregular verbs. Most likely the learner added the regular past tense morpheme *-ed* to the verb stem *writ-* instead of using the irregular form *wrote*. As a morphological error, we consider this type of misspelling a grammatical error. Another case of a spelling error that is typically covered by grammar checkers is that of easily confused word sets, homophones or near-homophones that learners and natives alike tend to confuse. A prominent example of this type is *its* and *it's* confusions. In this volume, we include grammar, usage and non-mechanical punctuation errors under the broad term of *grammatical error*, only distinguishing among them when called for.

1.4 PROMINENCE OF RESEARCH ON ENGLISH LANGUAGE LEARNERS

Most of the material cited in this volume is work that identifies and corrects errors made by learners of English. This is because most of the work in natural language processing (NLP) on error detection has dealt with errors produced by English language learners. English is the world's most commonly studied L2, so the need for tools is great:

> English, the first language of about 400 million people in Britain, the United States and the Commonwealth, has become the dominant global language of communication, business, aviation, entertainment, diplomacy and the internet. Over a billion people speak English as their second or foreign language.
> [Guo and Beckett, 2007]

There is also a growing urgency within the United States for students who are learning English as a second language. "America's 5.4 million Limited English Proficiency students represent the fastest-growing student population, expected to make up one of every four students by 2025" [NCLB, 2006].

There are significantly more NLP tools, such as part-of-speech taggers and parsers, devoted to English than to other languages. Due to the large number of native English speakers, large corpora of text for training data-hungry statistical systems are readily available, as are annotated data such as treebanks. As a result, advances in error detection in languages other than English have moved at a slower pace, or are more rule-based than statistical. Because of this imbalance, we have made every effort to seek out and cover research on errors made by learners of other L2s. We hope that this volume can contribute to the development of grammar checkers for learners of languages other than English.

1.5 SOME TERMINOLOGY

There is a distinction among English language learners between those who are learning English as a Foreign Language (EFL) and English as a Second Language (ESL). EFL is used to refer to people who are studying and learning English in a non-English speaking country, where the predominant language in their environment is not English. ESL is used to refer to non-native speakers who are living and studying English in a predominantly English-speaking environment. While the distinction is important for educators and sociolinguists, for our purposes we do not make the distinction, instead covering both groups under the term English Language Learner (ELL).

1.6 AUTOMATED GRAMMATICAL ERROR DETECTION: NLP AND CALL

Automated grammatical error detection for language learners falls under the broad category of Computer-Assisted Language Learning (CALL). The relationship between NLP and CALL has been a complicated and at times rocky one, fraught with unrealistic expectations and the trappings of "big AI." Unfulfilled expectations that NLP would provide classroom automation as a full-fledged conversation partner for students and targeted error feedback in language teaching have led to something of a backlash. In the aftermath of these inflated expectations, there has been a growing perception that NLP tools are just not able to deal with the full complexity of human language and should hence be avoided in language learning. For an introductory overview see Nerbonne [2003] and for a detailed discussion see Heift and Schulze [2007], especially Chapter 2. By focusing on the challenges and methods of automated grammatical error detection, we believe we can avoid these pitfalls. We will refrain from making any general statements or predictions about the general role of NLP in CALL. Instead, there are two modest claims that can be seen as guiding threads through this volume:

1. Modern techniques in NLP allow us to tackle a reasonable subset of learners' errors and to provide capabilities for detecting these errors, which can be useful to learners.

2. Automated error detection for language learners is an underexplored area for state-of-the-art NLP research that can potentially benefit the very large and underserved community of language learners—a rare opportunity.

1.7 INTENDED AUDIENCE

We hope that this volume can be of use to audiences from different backgrounds. Members of the EFL/ESL and CALL communities might be interested in the description of the state of the art in automatic learner error detection and correction. NLP practitioners might use the volume as an introduction to a small, but growing, area of research that poses unique and interesting challenges. Finally, students of NLP will find a number of open research questions to explore.

We are aware that audiences with these different backgrounds will also have very different kinds of background knowledge. In writing this volume, we have tried to strike a balance, avoiding oversimplification while at the same time not delving into minute technical detail. We assume that the reader has a basic knowledge of NLP concepts and basic machine learning terminology such as "parser," "classifier," "feature vector," and "language model," but we do not expect detailed knowledge of the underlying algorithms of, for example, a maximum entropy or voted perceptron classifier. Instead, we assume that readers will have access to a general reference such as Jurafsky and Martin [2008] or Manning and Schütze [1999] in order to get detailed information about NLP concepts that we do not cover. For an accessible introduction to machine learning strategies, we recommend Mitchell [1997], and for a more comprehensive and up-to-date introduction, Murphy [2012]. We also recommend Andrew Ng's free online course: Stanford Machine Learning.[1]

1.8 OUTLINE

In Chapter 2, "Background of Automated Grammatical Error Detection" we provide the historical context for automated grammatical error detection. We discuss both the general evolution of grammatical error detection and specific approaches to detecting learner errors.

Chapter 3, "Special Problems of Language Learners," outlines the special properties of learner errors, which are often very different from the errors that native speakers make because of the influence of the learner's native language. We go into some detail presenting three common errors in learner language: those involving prepositions, articles, and collocations.

In Chapter 4, "Evaluating Error Detection Systems," we take a close look at the evaluation of learner error detection systems, which is an important task that any practitioner in this area will face in presenting their results. We offer explicit suggestions for the design of a solid evaluation method, and we discuss different types of corpora for evaluation, as well as crowdsourcing approaches and strategies for measuring statistical significance of results. Typically, evaluation is based on annotated data, and we address this topic in Chapter 8. Readers who are interested in annotation may want to skip ahead to Chapter 8 after reading Chapter 4.

Chapter 5, "Data-Driven Approaches to Article and Preposition Errors," describes data-driven methods used to detect and correct article and preposition errors, the most studied error types. This chapter is organized along the types of data-driven methods used. At the end of the chapter, we present two current systems and illustrate their methodology.

Chapter 6, "Collocation Errors" turns to another prominent learner error, the misproduction of collocations. We discuss different word association metrics that are commonly used to identify collocations automatically from large corpora, and we address how this collocation information can be used in learner error detection and correction.

In Chapter 7, "Different Errors and Different Approaches," we focus on non-data-driven approaches to error detection and correction—including verb form errors, article errors, and preposition errors. We also cover data-driven approaches to punctuation errors, and methods for identifying whether the sentence as a whole contains any error.

Chapter 8, "Annotating Learner Errors," addresses issues and challenges encountered in annotating learner errors. There are now the beginnings of a growing consensus on this in the field. However, many issues remain unresolved.

Chapter 9, "Emerging Directions," highlights several areas in which progress has been made. This includes coverage of the two HOO shared tasks, the CoNLL 2013 shared task on grammatical error correction, ways in which machine translation techniques can be exploited, real-time crowdsourcing, and longitudinal studies about whether proofreading tools improve the users' writing quality.

[1]https://www.coursera.org/course/ml.

Finally, Chapter 10 outlines ideas and suggestions for future research. Appendix A contains an updated annotated list of learner corpora.

CHAPTER 2

Background

2.1 IN THE BEGINNING

The earliest widely used grammar checking tools, such as the *Unix Writer's Workbench* [MacDonald et al., 1982], were based on string matching rather than grammatical processing. Later systems, for example *CorrecText* (Houghton Mifflin Company) and *Grammatik* (Aspen Software) performed at least some level of linguistic analysis, and IBM's *Epistle* [Heidorn et al., 1982] and *Critique* [Richardson and Braden-Harder, 1988] systems ran full linguistic analyses using sophisticated grammars and parsers. Similarly, the Swedish *Grammatifix* checker [Arppe, 2000] developed by Lingsoft and the *Grammar Checker for Norwegian* [Johannessen et al., 2002] used Constraint Grammar [Karlsson et al., 1995] to produce a syntactic analysis of the input which made it possible to target a wide range of grammatical errors. This trend has continued until today. To the best of our knowledge, all of today's publicly available grammar checking programs (including Open Source systems like *AbiWord*[1]) are based on at least some linguistic that is enabled by hand-coded grammars or rules. Within the wider field of NLP, however, the dominance of rule-based approaches to grammatical analysis gave way in the 1990s to data-driven, statistical methods. Before the advent of large-scale annotated treebanks such as the Penn Treebank [Marcus et al., 1993] and the first statistical parsers trained from treebanks [Charniak, 1996; Magerman, 1995], parsers were based on large computational grammars that were written by linguists. After treebanks and other annotated resources became available, statistical approaches to grammatical analysis began to dominate the field, a development that is also reflected in automated grammatical error detection for language learners.

Grammars that are used in proofreading tools have one special property that is not shared by all traditional computational grammars. They need to be error-tolerant: parses for sentences with typical grammatical errors (subject-verb disagreement, for example) need to be generated as a necessary prerequisite for successful error correction. In addition, the parser needs to produce enough information in the final parse to indicate that the parse contains a violation of standard grammatical constraints of the target language. Large-scale computational grammars that do have this capacity include versions of Head-driven Phrase Structure Grammar such as the English Resource Grammar [Bender et al., 2004; Blunsom and Baldwin, 2006; Copestake and Flickinger, 2000], grammars based on Lexical Functional Grammar [Butt et al., 2002; Frank et al., 1998; Reuer, 2003], Constraint Grammar [Karlsson et al., 1995], and Augmented Phrase Structure Grammar [Heidorn et al., 1982].

---

[1]http://www.abisource.com/

Tolerance of grammatical errors in computational grammars has been achieved by a number of different mechanisms:

1. Over-generating parse trees and ranking them in order of grammatical compliance:

   Dini and Malnati [1993] generated parse trees that violate grammatical constraints but, when a constraint was violated, an error index was incremented. The best solution was the parse with the smallest index when the sentence was fully parsed, that is, the parse that satisfied the highest number of constraints in the grammar.

2. Imposing ranking constraints on grammatical rule violations:

   Ranking constraints involve adding rule-specific weights for certain violations [Heinecke et al., 1998; Menzel, 1990], including the restriction that a particular constraint can never be violated. This restricts the number of parse trees that are produced.

3. Introducing "mal-rules" that allow the parsing of specific errors in the input:

   Mal-rules were initially developed by Sleeman [1984] for errors in student math productions. An example of a mal-rule approach for language learners can be found in Schneider and McCoy [1998], whose system was developed for American Sign Language (ASL) signers. The authors examined essays written by ASL signers to identify common errors and then adapted a parser to identify those error types found in the essay collection. In writing by ASL signers, words that are not lexicalized in ASL are often omitted, such as articles "*I am transfer student*" and auxiliary verbs "*The boy happy.*" Schneider and McCoy then manually constructed rules to identify sentences that are missing these constituents. Bender et al. [2004] distinguished three different levels of mal-rules: syntactic mal-rules, lexical mal-rules that produce incorrect morphosyntactic realizations of verbs, for example, and lexical mal-rules that produce incorrect subcategorization information. They claimed that although mal-rules will always have limited error recall because they target very specific error types, they can still trigger feedback that is beneficial to a language learner if the targeted error types are frequent enough. A variation of the mal-rule approach was adopted in the *Scripsi* system [Catt and Hirst, 1990] where mal-rules were specifically designed to target L1 influences. More recently, Suppes et al. [2012] integrated an error correction feedback system based on mal-rules into an online course.

4. Relaxing constraints in feature unification:

   Hagen [1995] and Schwind [1990a, 1995] redefined unification so that the parse does not fail when two elements do not unify. Instead, the non-unified elements were recorded and subsequently used to produce user feedback. Douglas and Dale [1992] specified relaxations by making certain agreement constraints optional in their grammar. See also Vogel and Cooper [1995], Fouvry [2003], and for early work on grammar relaxation, Kwasny and Sondheimer [1981].

5. Parse fitting:

A computational grammar can be augmented by rules that try to "fit" together pieces of a parse tree when no complete parse can be constructed for the input. Jensen et al. [1983] proposed a fitting procedure that is activated when a bottom-up parser fails to produce a sentence root node. This procedure first finds a likely candidate for a head constituent, and then assembles remaining constituents into the head constituent. Mellish [1989] suggested running a top-down parser after a bottom-up parser has failed to come up with a successful analysis of the input. The top-down parser can examine the pieces of the parse provided by the bottom-up parser, making decisions about where the parse might have failed and what a complete parse might look like.

It is important to note that none of these approaches allow for the analysis of completely arbitrary ungrammatical input. Pre-identified likely violations (or classes of violations) of grammatical rules are built into the grammar rules, constraints, or feature algorithms, although the individual implementations vary considerably in their generality (see Heift and Schulze [2007], Chapter 2, for more details).

The problem of error tolerance is compounded in learner writing: the concentration of errors is much higher compared to native writing, where one can typically expect not more than one or two errors per sentence. Learner writing at a low proficiency level can be difficult even for a native speaker to parse and understand. Traditional linguistic tools such as parsers and part-of-speech taggers degrade in their performance when faced with such input, although they have been used in error detection and correction on learner writing (see the overview in Heift and Schulze [2007], sections 2.3 and 2.4). Some early examples include the *Automated German Tutor* [Weischedel et al., 1978], the *Scripsi* system [Catt and Hirst, 1990], the *Intelligent Language Tutor* [Schwind, 1988, 1990b], and *VP2* [Schuster, 1986]. Typically, these systems were built using relatively small grammars with a few very specific targeted errors. In general, applications for learner writing were limited and evaluations have been carried out only for small sets of errors in written answers to essay questions or reading comprehension questions given to students.

Instead of designing a specific proofreading tool for language learners, one could of course use an existing tool that has been developed for native speakers. When doing so, two problems become immediately apparent: these tools tend not to be very robust when confronted with learner language, and the targeted errors are only a subset of the typical learner errors. The latter is expected, given that native errors and non-native errors are quite different, as we will discuss in more detail in Chapter 3. Bolt [1992] examined the usefulness of eight proofreading tools (seven were commercial and one was academic) which he evaluated on a set of typical learner errors. His conclusion was that all eight programs underperformed on these errors and that they could even be of disservice to a learner.

Perhaps the most widely used grammar checker designed for native speakers is the one in Microsoft *Word*, which is described below in some detail as an illustration of the complexity of a broad-coverage rule-based proofreading system. The Microsoft NLP (MS-NLP) analysis system has been in use in Microsoft *Word* since 1997 and is arguably the world's most heavily used linguistic analysis system. It has also been employed in the Microsoft machine translation system [Quirk and Menezes, 2006].

The development of Microsoft's grammar checker began in 1991 with the implementation of a broad-coverage computational English grammar and analysis system at Microsoft Research. This work continued a line of research that had begun at IBM in the 1980s and was rooted squarely in the rule-based tradition [Heidorn et al., 1982; Jensen et al., 1983, 1993]. Work on the English grammar was followed within several years by grammar development in German, Spanish, French, Japanese, Chinese, and Korean. The computational grammars in the MS-NLP system are based on Augmented Phrase Structure Grammar (APSG) [Heidorn, 1975], which consists of sets of binary phrase structure rules. Constituents are represented as attribute-value data structures called *records*, which have a complex internal structure. Constituents on the left-hand side of these phrase structure rules can be annotated with linguistic restrictions on the constituents to be rewritten. The rewrite (right-hand side) of the rules can be annotated with any number of features and attributes. Rewrite rules are implemented in a language specifically developed for APSG, with an eye toward manageability for a trained linguist. The MS-NLP system provides several additional levels of linguistic analysis on the basis of this initial parse, resulting in a logical form semantic graph:

1. First, syntactic and semantic information is used to perform prepositional phrase and relative clause re-attachment in the syntactic structure.

2. This is followed by conversion to a dependency structure that then gets transformed into a full-fledged logical form where (intrasentential) anaphoric references and empty subjects are resolved and syntactic alternations such as active/passive are normalized.

3. Finally, sense disambiguation is performed on the logical form.

For both semantic reattachment and sense disambiguation, a semantic network called MindNet is used. MindNet is a large-scale semantic knowledge-base that was automatically produced by parsing dictionary definitions and examples. Dolan et al. [1993], Heidorn [2000], and Jensen et al. [1993] provide more details about the English analysis system, and Gamon et al. [1997] describe the approach to bootstrapping multilingual grammars from the English system. The parsers are supported by large-scale dictionaries with full morphological information in all targeted languages, and full semantic (sense and definition) information in a subset of the languages.

The ability to parse ungrammatical input in MS-NLP is achieved by two means. First, inviolable constraints on the left-hand side of rules are kept to a minimum (this corresponds to the strategy of over-generating parse trees mentioned above). Second, a parse fitting algorithm can produce a tree structure even if the initial parse has not succeeded. The resulting multitude of constituent and parse alternatives are scored heuristically (and penalized for violations of agreement and other grammatical errors), so that ideally the parse with the best possible structure (with the fewest penalties) will surface as the top scoring parse. Subcategorization constraints are not enforced: even an intransitive verb is allowed to combine with a noun phrase in object position. The resulting verb phrase will receive a penalty, however, based on the fact that an intransitive verb does not subcategorize for an object noun phrase. If despite this *relaxed parsing* the parser cannot generate a complete parse for a sentence (for example when the input is a sentence fragment), a *fitting* algorithm will identify the best candidates for large constituents and assemble them in a *fitted* parse.

Grammar development within the MS-NLP framework was greatly facilitated by high parsing speed (eight sentences per second on a state-of-the-art desktop at the time of development) and a suite of sophisticated grammar development tools. The combination of processing speed and visualization tools for parse trees and parse tree differences allowed results on tens of thousands of reference sentences to be computed and displayed within minutes, helping the grammar developer to assess the impact of a change in the grammar rules at short intervals during development.

The English *Word* grammar checker is designed to detect and correct typical errors made by native speakers of English, such as subject-verb disagreement. For this purpose, a special set of rules (*critique* rules) takes the MS-NLP parse (and in some cases the logical form) as input and tries to determine if one of the typical errors is present, and what the suggested correction should be. This error detection does not depend on sense-disambiguation or reattachment, and thus the semantic knowledge-base MindNet and the analysis rules it supports are not used in the product version of the grammar checker. The critique rules are themselves linguistically complex, balancing the need for robust error detection with the need to minimize false positives, which are notoriously annoying for users. Helfrich and Music [2000] provided an insight into the research and considerations that entered into the design and testing of the French, Spanish, and German grammar checkers for Microsoft *Word*.

To illustrate the parsing and critiquing in *Word*, consider the following sentence:
Three new text which deal with this problem has been written in the last year.
This example contains three errors:

1. The noun phrase *three new text* contains a plural quantifier and a singular head noun, resulting in number disagreement. Given this mismatch, it is not clear whether the noun phrase is singular or plural.

2. The relative pronoun *which* refers to *three new text* and the head of the NP (*text*) does not agree with the verb *deal* in the relative clause.

3. According to prescriptive grammar, the relative clause in this example is a non-restrictive relative clause and should be surrounded by commas.

The MS-NLP analysis first produces the parse tree shown in Figure 2.1. The semantic graph, called *logical form* (LF), that is shown in Figure 2.2 is produced from the parse tree. The LF normalizes the passive construction, assigning *three new text* to the deep object role of the predicate

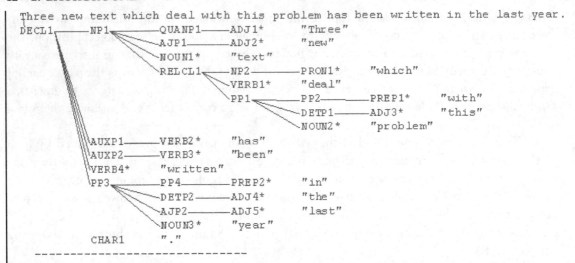

```
Three new text which deal with this problem has been written in the last year.
DECL1————NP1————————QUANP1————ADJ1*       "Three"
                    ↘AJP1————————ADJ2*       "new"
                     ↘NOUN1*       "text"
                      ↘RELCL1←————NP2—————————PRON1*     "which"
                              ↘VERB1*    "deal"
                               ↘PP1←————————PP2—————————PREP1*     "with"
                                         ↘DETP1————————ADJ3*      "this"
                                          ↘NOUN2*       "problem"
              ↘AUXP1————————VERB2*    "has"
               ↘AUXP2————————VERB3*    "been"
                ↘VERB4*   "written"
                 ↘PP3←————————PP4—————————PREP2*      "in"
                           ↘DETP2————————ADJ4*       "the"
                            ↘AJP2————————ADJ5*       "last"
                             ↘NOUN3*      "year"
           CHAR1      "."
```
- -

Figure 2.1: MS-NLP parse tree.

```
write1 (+Pres +Pass +Perf +Proposition +Resultat +T1 +Spact +Loc_sr)
↘Dsub————_X1
 ↘Dobj————text1 (+Pers3 +Sing +Mass)
          ↘LOps————three1 (+Quant +Plur +Num)
           ↘Attrib—new1 (+AO +Tme)
                  ↘deal1 (+Inf +Pres +Proposition +IO)
                     ↘Dsub————text1
                      ↘with————problem1 (+Def +Proxl +Pers3 +Sing +BndPrp +Count)
TmeAt————year1 (+Def +Pers3 +Sing +BndPrp +Count +Tme +Tme_sr)
      ↘Attrib   last1 (+AO)
```

Figure 2.2: MS-NLP logical form.

and produces an unspecified deep subject X. The relative pronoun *which* is also resolved as referencing the noun phrase *three new text*. On the basis of this analysis, the subject-noun phrase *three new text* and the relative clause are then marked with a feature *Numbdisagree* indicating the locations of disagreement (this feature is not shown in the figures). The error correction algorithm now proceeds through the following steps:

1. Since the noun phrase has internal disagreement, its number should be established first, before the verbs are checked against the number of the noun phrase. The plural quantifier *three* is a strong indication that the noun phrase was intended to be plural, so the head noun is changed to a plural and the suggested change for the subject is to rephrase it as the plural: *three new texts*.

2. If the user accepts this suggestion, a new parse of the revised sentence is created in order to check for subject-verb agreement. In this new parse, disagreement is detected between the 3rd person singular present tense verb *has* in the main clause and the plural subject, so a correction to the plural form of the verb is suggested.

3. The relative pronoun *which* refers to the subject of the main clause, and that subject has been changed to plural after the user accepted the suggested correction from step 1. Consequently, no change needs to be made to the verb *deal*; it agrees with the subject *which*. Finally, the relative clause is identified as a potential non-restrictive relative, based on the choice of relative pronoun. This information is used to suggest the insertion of a comma before and after the relative clause.

This example illustrates the complexity of a broad-coverage proofreading tool that was built on a powerful linguistic analysis component. As we saw above, however, such a system comes at a high price in terms of grammar expertise and needs to be designed carefully for the purpose of parsing erroneous input in order to detect and correct the errors.

We now turn to data-driven and hybrid approaches. While they avoid the problems faced by a rule-driven system, they face their own set of challenges.

2.2   INTRODUCTION TO DATA-DRIVEN AND HYBRID APPROACHES

One main advantage of statistical systems is that they avoid the problem of error intolerance that rule-based systems face. Statistical systems assign probabilities to word choices and sequences of words, therefore they can work with any sequence of words (and non-words), assigning high probabilities to sequences that have been observed during training or are at least substantially similar to seen strings, and assigning low probabilities to previously unobserved sequences and unknown words.

The idea of using statistical classifiers for grammatical error detection started as an offshoot of research in word sense disambiguation (WSD). At AT&T, Gale et al. [1992] pioneered the idea of using Bayesian classifiers for WSD. After this, work in statistical WSD flourished. The main pitfall in WSD research was that training and evaluating systems for WSD accuracy relied on corpora of polysemous words that were manually annotated to indicate which sense of a word is being used in each of thousands of sentential contexts. Creating these corpora was a slow, costly and error-prone process, but the research seemingly could not be done without it. David Yarowsky referred to this problem as the *knowledge acquisition bottleneck* and proposed a number of useful methods for avoiding the bottleneck so that researchers could continue with their experiments without waiting for annotated corpora. In one paper, Yarowsky [1994] avoided the bottleneck by proposing a task that is similar enough to word sense disambiguation but does not require manually annotated resources. He eliminated accents on words in Spanish and French and then predicted which tokens should contain accent marks. As an example, he took French sentences containing *côté* (coast) and *coté* (side) and trained a decision list classifier for each word. He then stripped all accents from held out *côté* and *coté* contexts and used the classifier to predict whether *cote* should be realized as *côté* or *coté*.

Extending this idea to a special class of spelling errors, Golding [1995] and Golding and Roth [1996] showed how decision lists and Bayesian classifiers could be used to detect errors resulting from common spelling confusions among words that sound the same (the homophones *peace* and *piece*) and words that sound similar (the near-homophones *desert* and *dessert*). They extracted contexts of correct usage for each member of a *confusion set* from a corpus and built models for each word's usage. A new occurrence of a confusable word was subsequently classified as an error when its context more closely resembled the usage model of another member of the confusion set than its own usage model. For example, if the context for a new occurrence of *desert* more closely matched the model for *dessert*, as in *His mother cooked a delicious desert*, the usage was identified as an error.

However, most grammatical errors are not the result of homophone or near-homophone confusions and to build models for each of them is an enormous task. For example, to use Golding and Roth's approach with article errors would require that a model be built for the article usage of each noun in the language. To extend the idea to prepositions, a model of preposition usage would also have to be generated for every noun/preposition pair, and so on. While the idea of separate models for each of a small set of homophones or near homophones is workable, it is not feasible to extend it to all possible grammatical errors.

During this same period, Knight and Chander [1994] developed a statistical method for correcting article errors in the output of machine translation systems. In this case, they used a decision tree classifier over lexical features to determine appropriate article usage. Articles were selected on the basis of similarity to the contextual features of the noun phrases in the training data.

Typically, the problem of error detection and correction has been looked at from one of two angles: the classification approach or the language modeling approach. In the classification approach to error detection, a classifier is trained on well-formed text to learn a model of usage for specific word classes such as prepositions and articles. The text is represented by features that are relevant to the error type. For example, while it is clear that a noun's countability is relevant for detecting article errors, it is likely not a feature that will be useful for detecting preposition errors. At application time, the classifier can detect if a particular use of a preposition or article, for example, is unlikely, given the information learned from the training data. Such unlikely word choices are good candidates for potential errors in the input. Much of the early work was done using decision trees, but several other types of machine learning classifiers such as maximum entropy and support vector machines are now more commonly used. All systems use the tokens in the immediate context of a potential error site as features, with the number of tokens actually used ranging from 3 up to 7 to the left and right of the error site. Other common features include part-of-speech tags and grammatical relations, such as "head noun" or "modifying adjective."

The idea of using language modeling for error detection, which goes back to at least Atwell [1987], is to build a single model of a language which represents correct usage. These statistical models are trained on large numbers of sentences and can assign a probability to a new sequence of words based on the counts of observed word combinations in the training corpus. In the context of error detection, the insight is that errors will most likely be located in an area of a sentence where the language model score is very low. In Chapter 5, we will illustrate the classification and language modeling approaches to preposition and article correction in detail.

Fortunately not all grammatical errors are so difficult to resolve that they require data-hungry machine learning methods. Indeed, some kinds of frequent grammar errors can be resolved with just a few lines of code and perhaps an exception list. For example, Gamon et al. [2009] describe the case of overregularized morphology of irregular English verbs—an error that language learners tend to produce. In *I eated an omelet for breakfast this morning*, the system simply needs a list of irregular verbs with "overregularized" forms and the appropriate irregular form. Sometimes such a simple heuristic works better than spell-correction systems that are designed for native speakers. In the case of *eated* in the previous example, Microsoft *Word*'s first suggestion is to replace it with *elated*.

Any robust grammatical error detection system will be a hybrid system, using simple rules for those error types that can be resolved easily and more complex machine learning methods for those that cannot. Such a system may even need to fall back on parsing, despite all of its inherent problems, as *n*-grams (sequences of tokens) frequencies will not be effective for errors that involve long distance relations. For example, it is hard to imagine how long-distance subject-verb agreement errors can be detected without having a high quality parse.

CHAPTER 3

Special Problems of Language Learners

The kinds of errors that language learners make overlap with the errors of native speakers. Native speakers and language learners alike are prone, for example, to misuse commas and semicolons, to confuse homophones, and to write run-on sentences. But language learners also make errors that occur comparatively infrequently in writing by native speakers. This is especially true for errors where usage is guided by complex rules that interact with one another, where few rules exist as in the case of collocations, or where they are influenced by the grammar of their native language. We describe, in detail, what a language learner (human or machine) must master in order to use articles, prepositions and collocations. We believe this is necessary background for any NLP research in detecting these errors.

3.1 ERRORS MADE BY ENGLISH LANGUAGE LEARNERS

There is a rich body of literature focused on how to define learner errors, error categories, and error taxonomies—topics that are beyond the scope of this volume. A thorough and fascinating review of this literature can be found in James [1998]. In this volume, we use the categories as they were defined by previous empirical learner error studies and by the designers of learner corpora.

Connors and Lunsford [1988] set out to determine what kinds of grammatical errors were made by college students in the United States. They analyzed 300 randomly selected student essays (which also contained the instructors' comments and grades) marking up all of the errors they encountered. They then compiled a list of all the errors, ranked by frequency. Spelling errors accounted for about one quarter of the total, dwarfing all the grammatical error categories, so they set spelling aside as a separate problem. They then took the 20 most frequently occurring of the 52 error types that were found and trained 50 volunteer analysts to identify these same errors in 3,000 college papers that were sent to Connors and Lunford by teachers across the United States. Columns 1 and 2 in Table 3.1 show the 20 most frequent errors and their ranks.

Donahue [2001] replicated this study, but with ESL students. He analyzed 200 randomly selected ESL proficiency tests using the entire Connors and Lunsford error classification. The rankings in Donahue's analysis are shown in the third column of Table 3.1. Although Donahue's study is small, it shows that the two populations exhibit quite a different pattern of errors. Whereas the three most frequent errors made by the U.S. college student population are (1) no comma after an introductory element, (2) vague pronoun reference, and (3) no comma in a compound sentence,

Table 3.1: Errors Made by U.S. College Students and by ESL College Students

the three most frequent errors in the ESL population are (1) comma splice (where two sentences are joined by a comma instead of a conjunction), (2) wrong word (as in *I *admiration/admire* my teacher*), and (3) missing word.

Note that half of the ten most frequent error types made by native speakers are negligible in the writing of the ESL population. This does not mean that language learners are more proficient in using these constructions, but rather that it is likely a case of avoidance behavior. The omission of a comma after an introductory element, in a compound sentence, or in a nonrestrictive clause requires the production of complex sentences. These complex sentences are likely attempted in the ESL placement essays only when the student is reasonably confident in their ability to construct them correctly, and are otherwise avoided.

The error categories in Table 3.1 were derived from frequent errors made by native speakers. For example, with article errors, there is a category for *missing article* but not for an *extraneous article* or a *wrong choice of article*. These likely wound up being counted as a *wrong word*. Thus, while the Donahue study gives us a picture of what errors are made by both native and non-native speakers, it gives only a partial picture of errors produced by language learners.

Beginning in 1993, Cambridge University Press, in collaboration with the University of Cambridge Local Examinations Syndicate (UCLES), began compiling the *Cambridge Learner Corpus* (*CLC*), a massive effort that involved identifying errors and inserting corrections in millions of words of text from the UCLES English for Speakers of Other Languages (ESOL) exams [Nicholls, 1999]. For a description of this and other learner corpora, see Appendix A. The version of *CLC* reported here has error annotations for a total of 20 million words. As with Connors and Lunsford, spelling is overwhelmingly the most frequent error and, following their lead, we excluded spelling errors from the numbers reported in Table 3.2. With spelling errors excluded, the most frequent error in the corpus is choosing an inappropriate open class word (noun, verb, adjective, or adverb). The next two most frequent error types in the corpus are preposition and determiner errors (these frequencies include all determiner and pre-determiner errors, not just the articles *a/an* and *the*).

The *National University of Singapore Corpus of Learner English* (*NUCLE*) [Dahlmeier et al., 2013] shows a similar pattern of errors made by non-native speakers. It consists of 1,400 essays written by college-level students at the National University of Singapore and corrections made by English-language instructors. The five most frequent errors are (1) wrong collocation/idiom/preposition, (2) local redundancies (*because of because*), (3) determiner, (4) noun number, and (5) mechanics.

It should be noted, however, that not all grammatical errors are equal. Connors and Lunsford [1988] were annotating essays that were already graded and include comments by the classroom writing instructor, so they calculated how many of the total errors were, in fact, corrected by the teacher. While an omitted comma after an introductory clause may be the most frequent error made by United States college students, the teachers corrected it only 30% of the time, so Connors and Lunsford concluded that the omitted comma wasn't perceived as being a

Table 3.2: Proportion of Errors in the *Cambridge Learners Corpus*

very important error. On the other hand, subject-verb agreement errors were corrected 58% of the time, so they were perceived as being more serious.

James [1998] describes one of his early experiments where he asked English teachers to rank error types according to their seriousness. The teachers had high agreement, ranking the two most serious errors as being word choice (*sky* versus *heaven*) and preposition errors.

Leacock and Chodorow [2003] distinguished those errors that are serious from those that are not by correlating the different error types that their *Assessment of Lexical Knowledge* (*ALEK*) system identified with essay scores on the Test of English as a Foreign Language (TOEFL). Essays written on the TOEFL exam are assigned a holistic score by two independent readers who use a 6-point scoring rubric. A high-scoring essay is well-organized and developed, and it contains few ungrammatical or non-idiomatic constructions. By contrast, a low-scoring essay is poorly organized and developed, and it contains many unclear sentences and grammatical errors. In their regression model, the most useful predictors of the TOEFL score involved subject-verb number disagreement (*My best friend *know/knows this guy*), ill-formed modal verbs constructions (*People would *said/say* …), ill-formed infinitive clauses (*…able to *began/begin a family*), and ill-formed participles (*their parents are *expect/expecting good grades*). These were followed by confused homophones (*some of *there/their grades*) and the confusion of morphologically derived forms *the *chose/choice I had to make*. Less costly errors involved problems with pronouns and with omitted punctuation. Error types identified by the system that had no correlation with the TOEFL score involved likely typographical errors: *he* when *the* was clearly intended, typing two articles in a row (*the the*), and typing *you* instead of *your* or *it* and *it's* confusion. Another error that did not correlate with the TOEFL score is the confusion between *have* and *of* following a modal verb, as in *I would *of/have gone*. This last is probably because it is an error that is also very commonly made by native speakers.

Leacock and Chodorow [2003] did not provide a definitive list of serious errors because they only measured the error types that *ALEK* was able to identify at the time, which did not include preposition and article errors. In order to examine the relation between the holistic essay score and article and preposition errors, we used a version of Educational Testing Service's (ETS) *Criterion* [Burstein et al., 2004], which does detect article and preposition errors. Results show significant correlations between both article and preposition errors and the overall TOEFL essay score.

3.2 THE INFLUENCE OF L1

It is well known that the kinds of errors a learner makes are, in part, determined by his or her native language. Swan and Smith [2001] is a guide for English language teachers that lays out what kinds of errors a language learner might produce based on their L1 for twenty-two individual native languages (e.g., Dutch, Greek, etc.) or language families (Scandinavian languages, West African languages). Each chapter was written by an expert in teaching English to native speakers of that language or group. This study is not corpus-based; it is anecdotal and informed by the authors' teaching experience, but many of the predictions can be confirmed by *CLC* corpus error frequencies. Swan and Smith note four major ways an L1 affects learner English:

1. Learning will be difficult if the L1 has no close equivalent for a feature. For example, native speakers of Japanese and Russian will have particular difficulty mastering the use of articles.

2. Learning will be facilitated if the L1 *does* have an equivalent feature. Swan and Smith point out, as an example, that native speakers of French or German will find the English article system comparatively easy to learn.

3. When two languages are similar, but not identical, there will be transfer problems, since those two languages will rarely have exact equivalents. Thus, French and German learners will make article errors where their L1's article system differs from that of English.

4. Speakers of unrelated languages will have fewer transfer problems than speakers of a closely related language, but they will make more errors due to the difficulty of complex English structures.

On one hand, when L1 and the target language are unrelated, learners have trouble because of the target language's novelty. This is the case when a speaker of an East Asian language tries to master the English article system. On the other hand, where L1 and the target language are similar, learners have trouble because of transfer problems. For example, a French speaker may write *depend of* in English instead of *depend on*. However, the kinds of errors made by the two groups of learners will not be the same.

3.3   CHALLENGES FOR ENGLISH LANGUAGE LEARNERS

Among the most *difficult* aspects of English for language learners to master are definite and indefinite articles (use of *a/an* and *the*) and prepositions. Combined, these small words account for 20%–50% of all grammar and usage errors in ESL writing [Bitchener et al., 2005; Dahlmeier et al., 2013; Dalgish, 1985; Diab, 1997; Izumi et al., 2003]. Article and preposition errors are also among the most difficult errors to recognize and correct automatically. For this reason, they are the focus of much of the work in grammatical error detection and correction for language learners. In the following two sections, we will take some time to describe, in detail, exactly why these two systems are so difficult to master for English language learners. Finally, we detail the difficulty in mastering collocations, which are also notoriously difficult to learn.

3.3.1   THE ENGLISH PREPOSITION SYSTEM

Preposition errors account for about 13.5% of the errors in the *Cambridge Learner Corpus* (not including spelling errors). Table 3.3 shows the proportion of sentences containing one or more preposition errors for eight L1s in *CLC*. Since all human languages contain adpositions (prepositions or postpositions), there will be interference or negative transfer no matter what the learner's

L1 may be. In addition to L1 transfer problems, prepositions are also difficult to learn because they perform many complex roles in English. Prepositions appear in adjuncts, they mark the arguments of predicates, they combine with other parts of speech to express new meanings as with phrasal verbs, and they participate in idiomatic expressions.

Table 3.3: Proportion of *CLC* Sentences Containing One or More Preposition Errors

Consider what an English language learner must master in order to correctly use prepositions in English:

Negative Transfer: While there is usually a most typical or frequent translation of a preposition from one language to another (e.g., *of* in English to *de* in French), in reality the correspondence between the prepositions of any two languages is many-to-many. As Diab [1997] noted, a single Arabic preposition can be translated using several different English prepositions (e.g., *in the garden, at home, on the campus*), and a single English preposition, in turn, can have numerous Arabic translations. This makes learning prepositions especially challenging, and it often results in negative transfer, especially for beginning ELLs who may simply choose the most typical translation when in doubt. For example, the error *driving in a high speed* (instead of *driving at a high speed*) incorporates the most common English translation of the preposition that would be used to express the same concept in Arabic.

Adjuncts: Prepositions are used in adjuncts to modify other elements of the sentence by expressing location (*at the beach*), time (*in summer*), and manner (*with a smile*), among other concepts. These phrases are generally optional and can appear at any of several positions [Pinker, 1994], thus increasing the variety of contexts in which a preposition appears. This greater variety of possible contexts makes the task of selecting the preposition more challenging for the learner. For example, the following six variations are all grammatical:

1. The children built the castle *at the beach in the summer*.

2. The children built the castle *in the summer at the beach*.

3. *In the summer* the children built the castle *at the beach*.

4. *At the beach* the children built the castle *in the summer*.

5. *In the summer at the beach* the children built the castle.

6. *At the beach in the summer* the children built the castle.

When we consider that *on the beach* may have been used instead of *at the beach* and that *during the summer* might have been substituted for *in the summer*, the variety and the complexity of the task facing the learner become all the more obvious. The choice of preposition in an adjunct is largely constrained by its object (*in the summer*, *on Friday*, *at noon*) and the intended meaning (*at the beach*, *on the beach*, *near the beach*).

Arguments of Predicates: Prepositions are also used to mark the arguments of a predicate, i.e., the participants in an event, state, or relationship [Pinker, 1994], such as the indirect object or recipient of an action (*He gave a book to Mary*), the logical subject or agent in the passive (*The book was written by Fred*), the instrument (*They ate the cake with a fork*), or the source (*Jane took the vase from the shelf*). Usually the event, state, or relationship is expressed by a verb, but sometimes it takes the form of an adjective (*He was fond of beer*) or a noun (*They have a thirst for knowledge*). A particularly common form of predicate is a nominalization, a noun derived from a verb, such as *remove+al*. With respect to how their arguments are marked, nominalizations have some properties of the verbs they are related to and some properties of nouns [Chomsky, 1970]. For example, in the sentence: They protested the removal *of the child from the classroom*, *from* marks the source argument of the nominalization *removal* in much the same way that *from* marks the source argument of the verb *remove*. However, *of* marks the object of the nominalization (*removal of the child*) but no preposition marks the object of the verb (*remove the child*). The choice of the preposition as an argument marker depends on the type of argument it marks (indirect object, source, agent, etc.), the word that fills the argument role (*put the book in the box*; *put the book on the table*), the particular word used as the predicate (*give a gift to Sally*; *bestow a gift on Sally*), and whether the predicate is a nominalization (*consideration of this matter*). Even with these constraints, there are still variations in the ways in which arguments can be expressed. Levin [1993] catalogs *verb alternations* such as *They loaded hay on the wagon* vs. *They loaded the wagon with hay*. These alternations mean that, depending on the verb, an argument may sometimes be marked by a preposition and sometimes not.

Phrasal Verbs: English has hundreds of phrasal verbs, which consist of a verb and a particle (most particles are also prepositions) that denote a meaning different from the verb alone. Compare, for example, the meaning of *give* and of *give up* or *give in*. For some phrasal verbs, the particle can appear before or after the direct object, as in *add up the numbers* or *add the numbers up*, while for others it cannot move from its position adjacent to the verb. To complicate matters, phrasal verbs are often used with prepositions (e.g., *give up on* someone; *give in to* their demands). Phrasal verbs are particularly difficult for non-native speakers to master because of their non-compositionality of meaning, that is, the whole is not the sum of the parts, and in many cases the whole seems completely unrelated to the parts. For example, what is contributed by the verb and by the word *on* in the combinations *get on* ("mount"), *hold on* ("wait"), and *catch on* ("understand")? The arbitrariness of the combined meaning forces the learner to commit these to rote memory.

Idioms: Non-compositionality is of course the hallmark of idioms, and prepositions play a prominent part in idiomatic expressions of all types. In a list of more than 1,800 idioms on a popular ESL website *Using English*,[1] 40% were found to contain a preposition. Not only are the meanings of the idioms largely unpredictable from the component words, but the selections of the words themselves are often at odds with their normal usage. For example, the preposition *in* appears more often than other prepositions with the object *house* (*in the house*), but *on* is used in the idiom *on the house*. Here too, the arbitrariness of word selection places a heavy burden on the learner.

Prepositional Phrase Attachment: Further complicating matters for the learner is the ambiguity that is present at every level of linguistic analysis. Structural ambiguity refers to the existence of two or more ways to assign syntactic relations, in this case between the prepositional phrase and what it modifies. In the sentence *I put the ring on the table*, the prepositional phrase *on the table* is clearly the destination of the action, but in *I put the ring on the table in the safe*, there are two possibilities. The phrase *in the safe* may be the destination of the action with *on the table* specifying which *ring*, or *on the table* may be the destination with *in the safe* specifying which *table*. This problem of deciding what a prepositional phrase modifies and other forms of structural ambiguity are extremely common in natural language. There is also lexical ambiguity, which in this case refers to the existence of multiple meanings of the prepositions themselves. Ravin [1990] describes five corpus-attested senses of *with* in the syntactic frame "Verb *with* Noun Phrase," including use (*eat with a fork*), manner (*view with anxiety*), alteration (*strike with fear*), co-agency or participation (*combine with others*), and provision (*furnish with supplies*). In fact, all prepositions have multiple senses (for example, the senses of *by* include agency, location, instrument (*by boat*), and time (*by noon*), among others) and, as noted above, languages differ in the ways they map prepositions to meanings.

3.3.2 THE ENGLISH ARTICLE SYSTEM

Unlike prepositions, and as predicted in Swan and Smith [2001], the writer's native language is often a good predictor of the likelihood of an article error. An examination of *CLC* bears out the prediction. Table 3.4 shows the proportion of sentences that contain one or more article errors for native speakers of four languages that have articles: German, Spanish, French, and Greek, and for four languages that do not: Chinese, Japanese, Korean, and Russian. The difference between the two language groups is statistically significant.

As with prepositions, English language learners are faced with a bewildering array of interrelated lexical, syntactic, and discourse rules to master. Many of these require the use of world knowledge, and each rule has its own set of exceptions.

---

[1]http://www.usingenglish.com/reference/idioms/list.php

Table 3.4: Proportion of Sentences with at Least One Article Error in the *Cambridge Learners Corpus*

Lexical features include the countability of the head constituent of a noun phrase which determines whether a noun can take the indefinite article. However, as Allan [1980] showed, noun countability is very complex. He defined a range of seven levels of noun countability preferences from fully countable nouns (*a car*) to strongly countable nouns (*The floors are made of oak* versus *an oak is in the front yard*), to weakly countable nouns (*I don't drink beer* versus *I'll have a beer*) to uncountable nouns (*equipment/*an equipment*). A noun's countability, however, can vary for a polysemous noun, where one sense can be countable while another sense is not, as in *read a paper* versus *write on a paper*. But constraints on the use of the indefinite article do not always depend on countability. They can also depend on the semantic class of the noun. Some classes of nouns, such as body parts, do not always take an indefinite article, as in *I looked him in the/*an eye*, even though they are fully countable.

Syntactic properties such as how a noun is modified or what kind of phrase it appears in can override countability. For example, some uncountable nouns, such as *knowledge*, can take the indefinite article when a prepositional phrase is attached, as in *a knowledge of English* but others cannot (*an/the equipment in the garden*). Also, when a fully countable noun is modified by a superlative adjective like *most* or *best*, or by an ordinal number like *first*, it takes a definite determiner: *a/the best car, *a/the first car*. When a fully countable measure or time noun is the object of *by*, it takes *the* as in *paid by *an/the hour* versus *worked for an hour* or *sold by *a/the gallon* versus *sold a gallon*.

Discourse factors also affect definiteness. The indefinite article is usually used to introduce an entity into a discourse while *the* is subsequently used to refer back to it (*I bought a book ...the book was expensive*), but there are many exceptions. For example, *The* house on the corner is for sale, is a very reasonable way to open a conversation [Quirk et al., 1985]. If the noun is being used generically, it will usually take the definite article when first mentioned (*the computer has changed our society*). Sometimes, the reference to an earlier entity is only indirect (*she found an umbrella but the handle was missing*).

World knowledge can be a factor in article selection. For example, *the* is used to introduce an entity into the discourse when it refers to something uniquely identified by the discourse participants (*the moon*) or their shared experience (*the last war*). These examples and many others are discussed in Quirk et al. [1985]. Some rules are highly constrained and require quite specific knowledge. *A* is used if a proper name refers to a company's product, but no article is used if it refers to the company's stock or the company itself (*He bought a Honda* versus *he bought Honda*).

3.3.3 ENGLISH COLLOCATIONS

Mastering conventional word combinations, or collocations, is another formidable task for any second language learner. For example, native English speakers know that the noun phrase *powerful computer* is preferred over *strong computer*, even though both are grammatically and semantically well-formed. Wray [2000] observes that:

> Knowing which subset of grammatically possible utterances is actually commonly used by native speakers is an immense problem for even the most proficient of non-natives, who are unable to separate out and avoid the grammatical but non-idiomatic sequences.

Not only are collocations arbitrary, but they are also pervasive, accounting for a large portion of the language that a learner must comprehend and produce. For example, Cowie [1991, 1992] reported that between 38% and 46% of all verb-object constructions in English journalistic prose (e.g., *hold an election, throw a party*) are collocations. Howarth [1998] found that about 33% of verb-object constructions in English social science texts are collocations.

The difficulty of learning collocations is well attested in the ESL/EFL research literature. Bahns and Eldaw [1993] investigated German advanced EFL university students' knowledge of English verb-object collocations. One group of 24 students took a fill-in-the-blank (cloze) test, and another group of 24 took a German-to-English translation test. On both tests, performance was only about 50% correct, suggesting that, even for advanced students, collocation is a major problem. Farghal and Obiedat [1995] reported that the average performance on a fill-in-the-blank collocation test of adjective-noun and noun-noun constructions was just 19% correct for 34 native Arabic-speaking English majors at a Jordanian university. They also found that, for native Arabic-speaking English teachers tested at the same university, the accuracy in translating collocations from Arabic into English was only 6%.

Collocation errors appear not only in fill-in-the-blank tests and translation exercises but in spontaneous writing as well. It is perhaps not surprising that learners' knowledge of collocations is highly correlated with measures of their writing quality. Zhang [1993] used a fill-in-the-blank collocation test and a writing test with native speakers and learners of English who were college freshmen. In both tests, native speakers significantly outperformed the non-native speakers. Al-Zahrani found a strong correlation between performance on a collocation test and the overall score on a writing test and on the TOEFL test for 81 native speakers of Arabic. Hsu [2007] found a significant positive correlation between the holistic writing score given by ETS's *Criterion* and the frequency and variety of lexical collocations in essays written by 62 Taiwanese college students. Wible et al. [2003] reported that lexical miscollocations were among the most prevalent error types marked by teachers in learner essays submitted through a web-based language learning system. Futagi et al. [2008] found that, in 300 randomly selected TOEFL essays, about 16% of the verb-object, adjective-noun, noun-noun, and verb-adverb constructions were collocation errors.

Not all types of collocations are equally difficult for English language learners. Those involving verbs seem to be most problematic. Nesselhauf [2003] reported that for a group of German university students studying English, the most frequent type of collocation error (accounting for 37% of the total) involved incorrect verb choice. Wible et al. [2003] extracted 177 miscollocations in Taiwanese students' English essays from learner data and found that 145 of the collocation errors were of the verb-object type. In all but three of these cases, it was the verb that was inappropriate. Liu [2002] analyzed 265 miscollocations in Chinese students' compositions in English and found 87% of the collocation errors to be of the verb-object type. Of these, 56% involved a synonym of the correct verb and another 38% were due to L1 interference, such as directly translating from Chinese (e.g., *eat the pill* instead of *take the pill*).

It is clear that collocations are difficult even for quite advanced learners, but what are the consequences of a learner having only limited knowledge of collocations? Choosing the wrong word can, in some cases, disrupt communication between writer and reader, but even in cases where the writer's intent is understood, the communication may be less precise than if a collocation had been used. Hill [2000] has argued that lack of competence in using collocations forces students to make more grammatical errors because they must use longer sentences to substitute for precise, compact expressions. Hill also argued that collocations allow writers and readers to communicate more efficiently since they can recognize collocations without processing them word-by-word. According to this view, one key to native-like fluency is having a large number of ready-made units immediately available in the mental lexicon to facilitate communication and reduce the cognitive load on both the writer and the reader. An important goal for natural language processing is to produce an application that can detect a learner's collocation errors and suggest the most appropriate "ready-made units" as corrections. This requires a means of identifying collocations and of measuring their quality.

3.4   SUMMARY

Almost every one of the usage rules for articles and prepositions has exceptions or subrules, and they interact in complex ways, which makes it much harder for English language learners to acquire the correct usage. Even worse, collocations appear to have no rules and therefore must be memorized. It seems quite amazing that *any* language learner can master these English constructions and astonishing that native speakers of English make relatively few errors using them.

The same types of complexity that human learners face must also be handled by automated systems designed to detect and correct errors. In the next chapter we turn to issues with evaluating error detection systems. The material in this chapter is technical, providing formulas needed to quantify system accuracy. In Chapter 5, we describe some of the systems that have been developed for article and preposition errors, and in Chapter 6, for errors involving collocations.

CHAPTER 4

Evaluating Error Detection Systems

In the first edition of this volume, we painted a gloomy picture of the state-of-the-art in evaluating error detection systems. At that time, unlike other areas of NLP, there was no shared task/repository to establish agreed-upon standards for evaluation. While it is still the case that researchers working in this field often find themselves using proprietary or licensed corpora that cannot be made available to the community as a whole, three shared tasks have now been sponsored so that researchers have the opportunity to compare results on at least some shared training and testing materials. The *Helping Our Own (HOO)* shared task was piloted in 2011 [Dale and Kilgarriff, 2011a] and was held again in 2012 [Dale et al., 2012]. Grammatical error correction was the featured task at CoNLL 2013 [Ng et al., 2013].

To illustrate the importance of having a shared task, consider the difficulty of trying to compare the performance of the preposition error detection systems reported by De Felice and Pulman [2008], Gamon et al. [2008], and Tetreault and Chodorow [2008a]. First, all three research teams used different evaluation sets: DeFelice and Pulman used *CLC*, Gamon et al. used *CLC* and the *Chinese Learners of English* (*CLEC*), and Tetreault and Chodorow used a proprietary corpus of TOEFL essays. To further complicate system comparison, they targeted different sets of prepositions: De Felice and Pulman focused on the nine most frequently occurring prepositions, Gamon et al. [2008] on twelve, and Tetreault and Chodorow on the most frequently occurring 34. In addition, all three teams tackled different aspects of the preposition problem. De Felice and Pulman developed a system for detecting preposition errors where the writer chose the wrong preposition. Tetreault and Chodorow developed a system that tackles wrong preposition choice errors as well as extraneous preposition errors, while Gamon et al. tackled all three kinds of preposition errors: choice, extraneous, and omitted. Finally, different evaluation metrics were used to report system performance and all three used different annotation schema and methods. De Felice and Pulman used accuracy and reported it separately for a set of prepositions annotated as being correct and a set annotated as being incorrect. Gamon et al. reported precision, while Tetreault and Chodorow reported both precision and recall.

For system development, it is necessary to have system-internal evaluation where the system's output is compared to a *gold standard* (the term used to refer to the correct or hand-annotated version). In deciding on what to use for a gold standard, several choices must be made—with the options most likely constrained by available financial resources. The first decision is whether to evaluate a system using well formed text or using learner writing. When the evaluation is based on the system's ability to predict word usage in well-formed text, it is not clear what the results are a measure of. Correcting a single error in text that is otherwise well formed is relatively uncommon in learner writing. If the evaluation is based on locating and correcting the errors in a corpus of learner writing, then it must be decided whether to evaluate manually in order to verify the system's output on a case-by-case basis, or use a pre-annotated corpus of learner errors, or to create one's own annotated corpus. The consequences of these decisions are discussed in this chapter.

That being said, as James [1998] documents, several studies show that people are not very good at recognizing and locating errors. For the remainder of this volume, we will accept the convenient fiction that it is possible for people to do these tasks well. We will address these issues further in Chapter 8, where we discuss methods for improving annotation and making the process more efficient.

This chapter provides an overview of the advantages and pitfalls involved in methods for evaluating grammatical error detection and correction: evaluation on well-formed writing, evaluation on learner writing, the use of multiple annotators in evaluation, and best practices for reporting results. Needless to say, evaluation is intricately tied to annotation. That is, how one decides to evaluate a system depends on (and influences) how one annotates errors in a learner corpus.

4.1 TRADITIONAL EVALUATION MEASURES

An error detection and correction system's performance is typically measured by its precision and recall, which are estimated using counts of true positives (TPs, also referred to as "hits"), false positives (FPs), and false negatives (FNs, also referred to as "misses"). A TP occurs when the system detects (flags) an actual usage error. In other words, what the writer has written differs from the gold standard, and the system agrees with the gold standard. This is shown schematically in the top row of Table 4.1, where X and Y represent different variables. For example, a system's performance is scored as a TP if it suggests inserting *a* before *walk* in the writer's sentence *I am going for walk this afternoon* and this matches the annotation. An FP occurs when a non-error (i.e., a correct usage) is flagged, such as when the system suggests deleting *a* from the writer's correct sentence *I am going for a walk this afternoon*. An FN occurs when the system fails to flag a usage error, which would be the case if the system found no error in *I am going for *walk this afternoon* but the gold standard did mark the error. The fourth possible outcome is a true negative (TN), where the gold standard indicates no error and the system agrees there is no error.

Precision is the proportion of flagged items that are, in fact, usage errors.

$$Precision = \frac{TPs}{TPs + FPs}$$

Table 4.1: *WAS* Evaluation Scheme (Adapted from Chodorow et al. [2012])

It measures how often the system is correct when it reports that an error has been found. Recall is the proportion of actual usage errors that have been flagged.

$$Recall = \frac{TPs}{TPs + FNs}$$

It measures the system's coverage, i.e., the fraction of errors that the system has detected. Researchers often combine precision and recall into an F-score, which is the harmonic mean of the two values.

$$F\text{-}score = 2 \times \frac{Precision \times Recall}{Precision + Recall}$$

Another measure of performance is overall accuracy, the number of correct cases divided by the total number of cases.[1]

$$Accuracy = \frac{TPs + TNs}{TPs + TNs + FPs + FNs}$$

However, accuracy can be misleading when evaluating error detection systems because, for any given construction, learners' error rates tend to be low, resulting in large values of TNs which dominate the calculation. For example, if preposition errors occur 10% of the time in a learner corpus, then even a baseline system that always treats prepositions as correct will have an accuracy of 90%.

Although precision, recall, and F-score are the most commonly used performance measures, they too can be misleading. Powers [2012] shows how they are affected by changes in the skewness of the data—the proportion of errors versus non-errors. For example, a system that performs no better than chance will nonetheless show an increase in recall when there is an increase in the proportion of cases annotated as errors in the gold standard (an increase in *prevalence*). Similarly, a system performing at chance will show an increase in recall when there is an increase in the proportion of cases that the system flags as errors (an increase in *bias*). This makes it virtually impossible to compare performance across different corpora with different proportions of errors and across different systems which generate error flags at different rates. What is needed

---

[1]Precision, Recall, F-score, and Accuracy are customarily reported as percentages, a practice that we will follow in the rest of this volume.

is a way of measuring and discounting the effects of chance agreement between the system and the gold standard.

To correct for chance agreement, Cohen [1960] developed the kappa statistic, which subtracts from the observed proportion of agreement, p_o, the proportion expected by chance, p_e, and divides this difference by 1 minus p_e:

$$\kappa = \frac{p_o - p_e}{1 - p_e}$$

If there are two category labels, *correct* and *error*, then p_o is the sum of the proportions of items assigned the same label by the scoring engine and the human annotator, over the k categories.

$$p_o = \sum_{i=1}^{k} p_{ii}$$

and p_e is the sum of the products of the proportions of each label's overall use by the system, $P_{(i.)}$, and the annotator, $P_{(.i)}$. That is, for each category i, the proportion of items that the annotator labeled i times the proportion of items the system labeled as i.

$$p_e = \sum_{i=1}^{k} p_{i.}p_{.i}$$

Values of kappa can range from 0 (no agreement) to 1.0 (perfect agreement).

Powers [2012] shows how measures, like kappa, which account for chance agreement provide a better picture of system performance and a more stable basis for system comparison than precision, recall, and F-score, which are affected by differences in the skewness of the data in the gold standard and in the system's output. The kappa statistic is also a very useful measure for reporting inter-annotator reliability, as described in Chapter 8. Landis and Koch [1977] present some guidelines for interpreting values of kappa in psychological research. They suggest ranges of $0.20 - 0.40$ for slight agreement, $0.40 - 0.60$ for moderate agreement, and above 0.60 for substantial agreement.

While kappa has advantages over precision, recall, and F-score, it is not without its own problems. The proportions of observed and expected errors must be computed over all cases, including TNs, but it is not always clear what should count as a case. For example, consider the detection of omitted articles. If the writer did not use an article, and the annotator and system agree that no article is needed, the system's output would be counted as a TN. How many TNs should be credited to a system that only suggests inserting *a* before *walk* in the sentence *I am going for *walk this afternoon*? The answer depends on which positions we consider to be possible sites for articles. If we consider the position before every word of the sentence to be a possible site, then the system has produced six TNs and one TP. Perhaps the set of possible sites should be restricted to positions immediately preceding noun phrases. There are three noun phrases in the sentence, *I*, *walk*, and *this afternoon*, but we can trivially eliminate the pronoun *I* as a possible site, and *this afternoon* already contains a determiner, which precludes the use of an article, so the number of TNs is, arguably, zero. The decisions that researchers make about what counts as a TN affect both accuracy and kappa [Chodorow et al., 2012]. This may be one reason why precision, recall, and F-score are more commonly used in evaluation.

Chodorow et al. [2012] observe that there is no single best measure of system performance; the usefulness of a measure will depend on the application and the goals of the researcher. For example, while kappa has advantages over precision, recall, and F-score for comparing systems, it cannot be used to provide the kind of information that is most important for deciding whether a system performs well enough to be put into actual operational use. It does not indicate how often the system falsely reports an error (precision) or the proportion of error instances the system detects (recall). There are other weaknesses as well. Kappa is known to favor correct classification of the less frequent class (in this case, the error class) over correct classification of the more frequent class (the non-error or correct usage class), though, for error detection, this might be viewed as a desirable property. Alternative measures of performance are constantly being proposed (e.g., [Powers, 2012]) to overcome deficiencies in the existing ones. Wagner [2012] notes that simply producing two accuracy scores, one for the actual non-error cases (TN/(TN + FP)) and the other for the actual grammatical errors (TP/(TP + FN)), provides numbers to describe system performance which are independent of the skewness of the data. He also demonstrates the value of accuracy curves, which are similar to the receiver operating characteristic (ROC), a graph that plots the true positive rate against the false positive rate when a threshold determining the classifier's bias is varied. In that regard, ROCs are similar to precision/recall curves, which plot the trade-off between precision and recall by varying a threshold, but, like kappa, the area under the ROC curve (AUC) is unaffected by skewness. In terms of classifier performance, AUC is a measure that can be interpreted as the probability that the classifier will assign a higher score to a randomly selected positive case than to a randomly selected negative case [Fawcett, 2006]. With so many evaluation metrics in use and others undoubtedly on the way, Chodorow et al. [2012] recommend that, whenever possible, researchers report the raw numbers on which current and future measures are likely to be based, i.e., the counts of TPs, FPs, FNs, and TNs. They also stress the need for researchers to be explicit about what they considered to be possible cases when counting TNs.

Our discussion thus far has assumed that there is a straightforward mapping between the writer's error, the annotator's correction, and the system's error flag. Often, this is not the case. For example, the sentence *Book inspired me* could be diagnosed and corrected by the annotator or by the system as an article error, a noun number error, or both. Each diagnosis has implications for how the error is counted and how the system's performance is recorded. Also at issue are the scope of the error and the linguistic status of the unit(s) involved. Does it encompass one word or two? Is it a lexical error, an error of morphology, or one of syntax? Furthermore, errors of different types can overlap or interact in other ways. For example, *Book inspire me* could be treated as *both* an article error and a subject-verb number agreement error, with the suggested correction of *The book inspires me* or *Books inspire me*. The decisions made in resolving these ambiguities will affect system evaluation and also the feedback that is given to the learner.

4.2   EVALUATION MEASURES FOR SHARED TASKS

The 2011 HOO Shared Task [Dale and Kilgarriff, 2011a] addressed some of the problems which result from the difficulty of mapping from annotation to system output. Three separate evaluations were carried out for *detection* (identification of an error), *recognition* (identification of an error's span and type), and *correction* (identification of at least one correction for an error). For detection, any overlap in the alignment of an edit (an insertion, deletion, or substitution) in the gold standard and an edit in the system output is treated as a TP. An edit in the system output that does not overlap any edit in the gold standard is an FP, and an edit in the gold standard that does not overlap any edit in the system output is an FN. With these definitions, precision, recall, and F-score can be calculated. To account for "optional" edits in the gold standard, detection is also measured with modified "bonus" versions of the precision, recall, and F-score formulas that award a TP for each optional edit, even if the system fails to detect it. For recognition, the second type of evaluation, the alignment of the gold standard edit and the system edit must be exact. For the third type of evaluation, correction, the gold and system corrections must match. The 2012 HOO Shared Task [Dale et al., 2012] focused on article and preposition errors. For the recognition evaluation, a new requirement was added for a case to be scored as a TP. In addition to exact alignment of the gold and system edits, both error labels (types) were also required to match.

Another approach to evaluation which mitigates some of the mapping problems is based on measuring the edit distance between the system's corrections and the gold standard, as for example in the edit distance algorithm called *MaxMatch* proposed by Dahlmeier and Ng [2012b]. Edit distance measures (EDMs) make it possible to define errors over sequences of words, and they can even handle fully overlapping errors, as when a spelling error and a number agreement error coincide (e.g., *A book inpire me*). Using an edit lattice, *MaxMatch* employs an efficient algorithm to search for a set of system edits that maximally matches the set of gold-standard edits. For CoNLL 2013, participants could submit multiple alternative sets of corrections and *MaxMatch* was extended to accommodate multiple gold-standard edits. This is especially useful as it is often the case that there are several valid corrections for a given error. (The issue of multiple valid corrections will be discussed in more detail in Section 4.4.)

The flexibility of EDMs comes at a price. By focusing on the strings that are being compared rather than on the sources of the errors or the types of units that are involved, EDMs make it harder to diagnose the nature of the errors and provide feedback to learners. And although EDMs can be used for calculations of precision and recall, as shown above, there does not seem to be a way to derive TN counts and compute kappas from them [Chodorow et al., 2012].

4.3   EVALUATION USING A CORPUS OF CORRECT USAGE

The easiest and fastest way to evaluate a system is to use text that is largely error-free, such as newspaper or newswire corpora, which are freely available in vast quantities. The assumption behind evaluating on newspaper/newswire text is that these texts have been written predominantly by native speakers and have been both copyedited and proofread, so it presumably represents correct usage. Of course, some errors do occur in these corpora, but they are relatively infrequent. Using well-formed corpora, an error can be counted each time the system predicts a token that is different from the choice observed in the text. Similarly, a prediction can be counted as being correct each time the predicted and observed choice is the same. For example, consider the sentence:

The marching band came past post office.

If a proofreading system predicts inserting *the* before *post office*, then a correct prediction is counted whereas if the system predicts either *a* or the zero-article, then an error is counted.

Edited text provides a vehicle for evaluation that is fully automated, rendering system accuracy results instantaneously. Evaluation on correct usage is especially useful during system development, where one can check how any modification affects system accuracy—with one caveat: evaluation on well-formed text makes the assumption that whatever occurs in the original text is the only possible correct form. Since this assumption is false, precision is underestimated. For example, when evaluating their preposition error classifier, Tetreault and Chodorow [2008b] examined the system's false predictions and found that, in many cases, more than a single preposition could appropriately be inserted into the sentence. Both *of* and *in* are appropriate prepositions to use in the following sentence:

They thanked him for his consideration ____ this matter …

However, if their system predicted *of* and the original contained *in*, that prediction was counted as incorrect.

Nevertheless, testing on correct usage data is useful for comparing results among different systems even when, as is almost always the case, they evaluated on different well-formed corpora. Such comparisons are based on the assumption that the distribution of, for example, articles will be roughly the same for the different samples of edited text. This assumption, however, is more likely to be true for articles than it is for pronouns, where newswire corpora will contain relatively fewer first person pronouns than will a corpus of fiction. Therefore the value of comparing systems on different sets of edited data needs to be considered on a case-by-case basis.

Evaluating on edited text also artificially inflates precision because the context surrounding the potential error site is error-free, whereas learner writing can be, and often is, riddled with errors. To get an estimate of how performance differs on well-formed versus learner writing, we carried out the following experiment. All of the *CLC* sentences that contained article and preposition errors were extracted and used to create two test sets: a "corrected set" where, with the exception of the targeted error, all of the other errors flagged in the sentence were corrected, and the "original set" where none of the other errors were corrected. Errors that were marked as being spelling errors, however, were corrected, so the uncorrected sentences were partially cleaned up. Upon testing the corrected set with Microsoft Research's *ESL Assistant* error correction system, the precision for article errors increased 10% and recall rose 4%. For preposition errors, precision increased 8% and recall increased 3%. Even so, these results underestimate the difference between evaluation on well-formed text and learner writing because learner writing is much less formulaic and idiomatic than that of newspapers. Learner writing contains many unusual lexical choices for open-class words that, while not being errors, are not as idiomatic as, for example, the *New York Times*. Sparse data are even sparser when using non-idiomatic writing.

As useful as evaluation on correct usage may be for system development and comparison, well-formed corpora have little resemblance to learner writing. System evaluation on well-formed data says little about how the system will perform with the targeted audience, language learners.

4.4 EVALUATION ON LEARNER WRITING

Every day, large quantities of language learner writing are produced and corrected all over the world, but very little of that information is preserved or archived in electronic form. However, a number of learner corpora have been developed, some of considerable size, and some of these also contain rich error annotations. Appendix A is a listing of learner corpora that are currently available—some are freely available and others need to be licensed. These corpora can be used for a number of purposes such as producing the ELL error analysis in Chapter 3, training machine learning systems that will be discussed in Chapter 5, and evaluating systems.

However, evaluation on learner writing presents a new set of problems because the error categories are not as clear-cut as they are when evaluating performance on correct usage. The classification for well-formed textual data is quite straightforward—even if native speakers do occasionally disagree. With learner productions, instead of being able to make a single decision about one construction in an otherwise perfectly formed sentence, we are now faced with contexts that are likely to contain many errors. There is a sizable neutral space between making a single change that either creates a well-formed sentence or introduces an error. Neutral in that the change neither improves nor degrades the original. For example, an error might be correctly identified but the correction is wrong (e.g., *a* is inserted instead of *the*), another error (either grammatical, semantic, or spelling) occurs in the context (e.g., an article correction has been triggered by a preposition error), or both the original and the suggested rewrite are acceptable.

4.4.1 VERIFYING RESULTS ON LEARNER WRITING

When learner writing samples have not previously been annotated for grammatical errors, each error flag produced by the system must be evaluated, or verified, manually. This verification is a process that is slow, tedious, and costly in terms of time and therefore money. It is also prone to error due not only to lapses in concentration but also to disagreement among evaluators.

To account for and classify the neutral space that is introduced by evaluation on learner productions, Gamon et al. [2008] used the classification system in Table 4.4.1 when reporting system results. Whereas evaluation on well-formed usage maps only to category 1 (*Correct Flag*) and category 5 (*False Flag*) in Table 4.4.1, approximately one-third of the error flags for both articles and prepositions reported in Gamon et al. [2008] were distributed among categories 2 through 4. Although these categories do not correct an error, they are arguably neutral or even positive, because they at least point to a problematic area or suggest an alternative way to express a concept. Tetreault and Chodorow [2008b] provide instructions in their annotation protocol for recognizing and annotating environments that will map to category 4 (where there is another error in the context).

Table 4.2: Error Categories Used in the Verification Approach (Adapted from Gamon et al. [2008])

When manually evaluating results, it is preferable, though not always possible, to use more than one person to evaluate/annotate a subset of the flags in order to be able to report inter-annotator agreement, which can act as an upper bound on system performance. With some kinds of errors, such as overregularized verb inflection (*I *sleeped/slept*), inter-annotator agreement will be high—with annotator disagreement largely limited to lapses in concentration. With other error types, especially preposition usage, different native English speakers within the United States may disagree depending on factors such as age and geographical location. For example, three of the authors of this monograph find the use of *for* in *I'm excited for dinner* terrible, preferring *about*, but the fourth author (along with one author's two twenty-something daughters) use *excited for* all the time. We're guessing that the difference is age related. Tetreault and Chodorow [2008b] report that for the annotation of preposition errors "using a single rater as a gold standard, there is the potential to over- or under-estimate precision by as much as 10%."

4.4.2 EVALUATION ON FULLY ANNOTATED LEARNER CORPORA

There are clear advantages to evaluating on a preexisting fully annotated learner corpus. The corpus is annotated by trained experts, which takes the onus of evaluation away from the researchers. Theoretically, all of the errors are identified and coded as to the error type, which makes it possible to calculate recall. System developers who have access to an annotated corpus can easily compute precision and recall when, for example, a new feature is added, and this is far more informative than performance results based on well-formed text. Unfortunately, as mentioned earlier, many of these corpora are often proprietary or expensive or too small to provide reliable statistics. Furthermore, the reliability of the annotation may be an issue.

In the remainder of this section, we discuss those issues that arise upon using an annotated corpus for system evaluation. However, the properties of an annotated corpus depend crucially on choices made when the corpus was being designed. Chapter 8 details the many and complex issues surrounding the process of creating annotated corpora. So, while this section informs the *consumer* of annotated corpora, Chapter 8 will inform those who will create their own annotated corpus of learner language.

Some of the annotated learner corpora listed in Appendix A are *fully* annotated (for example, *CLEC*). However, these corpora were not created to be used for evaluating error detection systems, so that even high quality error-annotated corpora pose challenges for system evaluation. To be useful for evaluation, an error-annotated corpus needs to identify an error *and* provide a correction, which raises the question: How does the annotator know the original writer's intent? In addition, there is often more than a single way to correct an error, but error-annotated corpora typically provide only a single correction. Annotator agreement for some error types is problematic. Annotation can be tedious and prone to error, but there are also genuine cases of disagreement. Many of these problems could be identified and resolved if each sentence were annotated by more than one annotator. Similarly, constructions on which annotators disagree could be identified. But having multiple annotators, which permits a measurement of reliability, is expensive and rare. In fact, we are not aware of any error-annotated learner corpus where all of the errors have been analyzed by more than one annotator.

In order to avoid some of these problems, work such as Han et al. [2006] and Tetreault and Chodorow [2008b] have developed corpora that each target a single error type. For example, one corpus is dedicated solely to article errors and another solely to preposition errors. Where appropriate, these corpora also provide more than one correction if more than a single preposition or article is acceptable in a given context. These are described in Chapter 8.

When Gamon [2010] evaluated a preposition classifier on a fully annotated learner corpus, based on *CLC* annotations, he found that precision was much lower than the precision that had previously been calculated based on the verification approach. Therefore, he decided to have a subset of the false positives manually verified. When calculating precision against *CLC*, counting a TP only when the error in the corpus was flagged as being a preposition error and the system's suggestion agreed with the annotator's correction, he reported 32.9% precision. With verification, the neutral evaluation categories 2–4 from Table 4.4.1 emerged, as well as two additional categories:

1. The classifier corrects an error that was either not annotated in the corpus or, more often, corrects it differently than the annotator. As an example, consider the context:

   …which could lead *to accident*.

   This can be flagged as either a noun-number error (*lead to accidents*) or as an article error (*lead to an accident*). In this case, if the annotator flagged it as a noun-number error, the system's suggestion to insert *an* would be counted as a false positive.

2. There is an error in the corpus that *is* flagged as containing the targeted error, for example a preposition error, but the annotator and the classifier chose different prepositions to fix the error—when both corrections are acceptable. For example, *by* might be replaced in the corpus with *to* while the system deletes *by* in *You are very near by my town*. So, if the preposition classifier suggests deleting *to* before *town*, it would be counted as a false positive.

When Gamon [2010] counted only cases where the suggested rewrite degraded the quality of the sentence by introducing an error, he reported 85.3% precision. Thus, while using an error-annotated corpus for system development is extremely valuable (for example, the relative numbers can show whether the classifier's performance is improved or degraded by the addition of a new feature), it will underestimate the actual precision and recall.

Nevertheless, many studies report results on fully error-annotated corpora. These include Izumi et al. [2004a], Lee and Seneff [2008], De Felice and Pulman [2009], Gamon [2010], and Dahlmeier and Ng [2011a]. As a rule, these studies report results with low precision and recall (except for Lee and Seneff [2008], which examined a restricted error set). So, when evaluating on an error-annotated learner corpus, it must be kept in mind that the system's actual precision and recall are probably higher than the reported results.

Even when researchers have used verification or have evaluated on fully annotated corpora, they also, for ease of comparison with other systems, report results on well-formed text. However, when they report results based on an error-annotated learner corpus, they are likely do some additional verification, as did Tetreault and Chodorow [2008b] and Gamon [2010]. Also, recall the findings of Tetreault and Chodorow [2008b] that system results can vary by as much as 10% depending on who is evaluating the system output.

4.4.3 USING MULTIPLE ANNOTATORS AND CROWDSOURCING FOR EVALUATION

One way to improve the reliability of manual evaluation is to have multiple annotators evaluate the same error flags and then discuss discrepancies in judgments and produce a gold standard *adjudicated* set. The advantage of this approach is that each construction is vetted and sometimes discussed by more than one annotator. However, this obviously requires more time and resources. Another method is to treat each annotator's evaluation as a gold standard, evaluate the system on each set, and report the results. This shows the range of the system's performance.

When multiple annotators are used, inter-annotator agreement should be reported using the kappa statistic. Cohen's kappa (see Section 4.1) can be calculated for any number of categories, but it is limited to two annotators. A generalized form of kappa was developed by Fleiss [1981] and can be applied to situations in which there are any number of annotators.

A main issue for the first HOO shared task was the cost of annotation:

> Overall, the biggest challenge we face is the cost of data annotation. Identifying errors and proposing corrections across such a wide range of error types is a very labour intensive process that is not easily automated, and is not amenable to being carried out by unskilled labour. [Dale and Kilgarriff, 2011a]

However, as is described in Chapter 8, Tetreault et al. [2010a] experimented with using crowdsourcing to annotate errors and found that it can be used to cheaply and accurately annotate preposition errors. However, no one has yet published results using crowdsourcing to annotate learner writing that has multiple error types—which was the case with the HOO shared tasks.

Annotator disagreement has traditionally been considered as a negative, with an assumption that, in the case of disagreement, one of the annotators is wrong. Madnani et al. [2011] showed that, in the context of crowdsourcing, annotator disagreement is a valuable source of information. When annotators are instructed to make a grammaticality judgment on all cases of preposition usage, for example, they are being given an unreasonable task. While many cases are clear-cut and yield high agreement among the annotators, there are others that are borderline, resulting in much less consensus, and still other cases where the annotators may be almost evenly split in their judgments. Instead of simply computing a majority vote of correct or incorrect, Madnani et al. [2011] used agreement proportions to weight precision and recall, which they consider to be fairer and more stable performance indicators than unweighted precision and recall.

Madnani et al. [2011] also used annotator consensus to compare different systems. Using 20 crowdsourced annotators, they suggested sorting errors into three agreement bins: one where the annotators have very high consensus (for clear-cut errors), a second where agreement is between 75% and 90% (for borderline cases), and a third for cases where the annotators have low consensus (instances of genuinely different judgments). Upon plotting precision and recall for each of the bins for each system, the curves allow system comparison on high-, medium-, and low-consensus errors. Madnani et al. [2011] argued that measuring performance on cases that have roughly equal levels of annotator consensus is a better way to compare systems. Ideally, these plots should be used when the systems are being evaluated on the same corpus, but they can also be used for comparisons on different learner corpora.

4.5   STATISTICAL SIGNIFICANCE TESTING

In a recent paper, Berg-Kirkpatrick et al. [2012] argued that NLP evaluations should (almost) always include statistical significance tests of differences in system performance. Unfortunately, significance testing has not been universally reported in the grammatical error detection literature. The reasons for its omission are no doubt the same as those for other branches of NLP: Often the test data are of very limited size, and the performance metric, such as the F-measure, is not normally distributed. Berg-Kirkpatrick et al. [2012] used the paired bootstrap sampling method [Efron and Tibshirani, 1993] to overcome these obstacles. The bootstrap makes it possible to estimate confidence intervals and a *p*-value for hypothesis testing with limited data and almost any evaluation metric.

Suppose that we have *n* cases in our test corpus and two grammatical error detection systems, A and B, which we wish to compare. We run A and B on the test cases, compute the F-measure for each, and then calculate the difference, $F_A - F_B$. This is the actually observed difference in our test data. Next, we randomly draw a sample of *n* cases from our test corpus, *with replacement*. In effect, we are using the test corpus as a proxy population from which to draw new samples, known as bootstrap samples. We run A and B on the cases in the bootstrap sample, compute the F-measure for each system, and then calculate the difference between the two F-measures. This process of drawing a new bootstrap sample and calculating the F-measure difference is then repeated many times, resulting in a distribution of F-measure differences that can be ordered from smallest to largest. For a 95% confidence interval, we can use the values that separate the lowest 2.5% and the highest 2.5% from the rest of the distribution. For hypothesis testing, we can see if our actually observed difference is smaller than the interval's lower limit or greater than its upper limit.

In their wide-ranging study, Berg-Kirkpatrick et al. [2012] used the bootstrap to evaluate system differences for constituency parsing (F-measure), word alignment (error rate), summarization (ROUGE score), and machine translation (BLEU score). The researchers also addressed the reliability of significance testing for constituency parsing when the test data are from similar domains (different sections of the WSJ corpus) or from different domains (WSJ and the Brown corpus). Unfortunately, there was considerable loss of reliability in the different domain condition leading Berg-Kirkpatrick et al. [2012] to conclude that "achieving a p-value near 0.05 on section 23 (of WSJ) provided no information about performance on the Brown corpus" (p. 1003). As of this writing, comparable experiments have not yet been performed for grammatical error detection/correction. (However, see Cahill et al. [2013b] for a study that uses bootstrap sampling to calculate the significance of performance differences of systems based on the same statistical classifier but with various amounts of training data, types of features, and kinds of learner test corpora.)

4.6   CHECKLIST FOR CONSISTENT REPORTING OF SYSTEM RESULTS

Different researchers make very different assumptions when reporting system results. This makes comparison between systems not only difficult, but also potentially misleading. Byron [2001] proposed a reporting standard for evaluation of pronoun resolution systems that clarifies the details of a study's training and test data and explicitly shows how performance measures were computed. In the same vein, we would like to suggest reporting practices for grammatical error detection:

1. Report TPs, FPs, FNs, and TNs whenever possible. This will enable readers to calculate measures based on those four counts, such as accuracy, precision, recall, F-score, prevalence, bias, and kappa, even if you choose not to report all of these measures in your paper. It will also enable future readers to apply yet-to-be-developed evaluation metrics to your data.

2. Be explicit about the usage errors your system targets. For example, for preposition correction, list all of the prepositions it targets.

3. Be explicit about what usage contexts have been included/excluded. For example, if a noun phrase already has a non-article determiner, such as *some*, this automatically precludes adding an article. When reporting on article error detection, make it clear whether you are counting non-insertion of articles in these noun phrases as a correct prediction. Such choices will affect the TN count and, therefore, the values of accuracy and kappa.

4. When reporting F-scores, give precision and recall, or provide the counts from which precision and recall can be calculated. The F-score can be difficult to interpret in the context of grammatical error detection because it assumes that precision and recall are equally important and gives them equal weight. Most researchers, however, consider precision to be much more important than recall in grammatical error detection because they fear an adverse effect on the learner if the system produces too many false positives. There is, in fact, some empirical evidence to justify this concern based on a study by Nagata and Nakatani [2010], which is described in Chapter 9.

5. Describe the properties of your test corpus, including the population from which the learners were drawn, their proficiency levels, the size of the corpus, and the frequencies of the error types.

6. It is best to be cautious when comparing systems based on their F-scores since this measure is sensitive to skewness in the data, which can be particularly problematic when the systems are tested on different corpora. If possible, use kappa for comparisons instead, or provide enough information so that prevalence and bias can be calculated for each system's evaluation.

7. It is always preferable to use multiple annotators. When doing so, report inter-annotator kappa along with agreement.

8. Whenever possible, test system performance differences for statistical significance.

Supplying more information about how the research was carried out, what contexts are being identified, and the characteristics of your training and test corpora is always better than supplying too little. This enables the correct interpretation and replication of your work.

4.7 SUMMARY

While numerous measures have been developed to evaluate system performance, no single measure is best for all purposes, and not all forms of evaluation can supply the information needed to calculate all of the measures. For example, the verification method can be used to estimate precision on learner data, but not recall or TNs. Another important consideration for evaluation is how to measure performance when targeted errors span multiple words or when different types of errors overlap. EDMs promise a way to handle these complexities but have their own limitations. The quality of evaluation also depends upon reliable annotation, which is often difficult to obtain, especially for word usage errors. Multiple annotation can reduce unreliability, and crowdsourcing has proven to be a fast and inexpensive way to obtain multiple judgments. It also affords the opportunity to evaluate performance on a continuous scale rather than a discrete one.

Evaluation should provide results that are generalizable. In this regard, calculating statistical significance can help, but usually not when it comes to generalizing from one test corpus to another. For example, evaluating on well-formed text is fast and cheap, but it does not predict how well the system will perform on learner writing. Another factor affecting generalization is how the test corpora are annotated. Measuring performance on fully annotated learner corpora provides both precision and recall, but when the actual cases of mismatch between the system's output and the annotation are inspected manually, they often turn out to be evaluation "mistakes" that cause true precision and recall to be underestimated. Ideas for overcoming some of these problems are discussed in Chapter 8.

With a reliably annotated corpus of learner errors, it is possible to estimate the accuracy of a system, but that still leaves an important, arguably the *most important* question, unanswered: Does this system help language learners improve their writing skills? To answer this question, we need to look at actual users interacting with an operational system and see how it affects the quality of their writing. That is, we need user studies, which will be discussed in Chapter 9.

CHAPTER 5

Data-Driven Approaches to Articles and Prepositions

In this chapter, we examine error detection and correction as applied to article and preposition errors. There are two reasons why we focus on these two error types. First, as we have seen in Chapter 3, prepositions and articles are notoriously difficult for English learners to master, so they represent a large subset of learner errors. Second, the vast majority of work in automatic grammatical error correction has been on the prediction of articles and prepositions in text. Much of the work on other error types (see Chapter 7) has borrowed or adapted approaches originally used for articles and prepositions. By focusing on these two error types, the reader can gain a greater understanding of the range of data-driven techniques that are employed for error correction as a whole.

Articles are ideal targets for automatic error detection because they are among the most frequent English learner errors. Research typically focuses on the use of the indefinite and definite article as well as the zero or null article. Prepositions are more challenging targets for automatic error detection than articles, in part because there are more of them. English, for example, has over one hundred prepositions. Fortunately, there is little need to model all prepositions since the ten most frequent ones account for 82% of all the preposition errors in the *Cambridge Learner Corpus*. This makes it possible to achieve very reasonable coverage of learner errors by modeling only a small subset of them. Systems have been trained on subsets of prepositions ranging from just a handful to several dozen.

We will attempt to give a thorough overview of the literature, with particular attention to the technical approaches and the information used to detect and correct article and preposition errors. However, given the massive body of work dealing with those two error types, much of which has been published since the first edition of this volume, we focus on the key papers in the field. The 2012 HOO Shared Task focused on articles and prepositions, but we discuss it in Chapter 9 rather than here so that it can be presented along with the 2011 HOO and 2013 CoNLL Shared Task in our coverage of those three shared tasks as a whole.

Data-driven approaches to article and preposition errors can be classified in terms of

- the kinds of features they extract from the training data

- the training data they use

- the kinds of models they construct

Features derived from the context in which the target word occurs can include lexical items, part-of-speech tags, parse features, and semantic information. Training data can consist of well-formed text, corpora with artificially introduced errors, and learner corpora with annotated and corrected errors. Finally, models can be based on statistical classifiers, *n*-gram statistics/language modeling, and some novel techniques that fall outside these categories.

Naturally, there is sometimes overlap between methods; some projects could be discussed under several headings in this chapter and researchers often combine methods into a hybrid system. Thus the categorization is not as clear-cut as the organization of this chapter might suggest. We will not be able to go into much detail for many of the systems and it will be impossible to give all systems equal treatment. Still, we hope that this presentation of the material facilitates the overview of a diverse field.

In the second part of this chapter, we present in greater depth two large-scale systems which either have been or are currently being used operationally.

5.1   EXTRACTING FEATURES FROM TRAINING DATA

As one might expect, the information used by different systems is diverse, but in general it can be grouped into the following categories:

1. Data-driven systems often use *token context* information: for each point in a sentence where a decision about a preposition or article needs to be made, the information about a number of tokens to the right and/or left is extracted and used to train a classifier. There is considerable variation, however, in the number of tokens that are extracted from the right and/or left context, and whether the tokens are extracted individually or as longer *n*-grams. Token sequence probabilities can be assessed through techniques such as language modeling, web *n*-gram corpora, or even through the direct use of a web search engine.

2. A more complex source of information is *syntactic context* information. Based on one or more linguistic analysis components, the following pieces of information are commonly used:

   (a) *Part-of-Speech (POS) information* can be used in a number of ways. Once a part-of-speech tagger or a parser has assigned part-of-speech tags to all the tokens, this context can be extracted in a manner similar to the token context. Additionally, part-of-speech tags allow one to determine what the head of a noun phrase or verb phrase is (in some cases with the additional help of specific head-finding rules), and this information can be used to extract not just any token from the context but to focus on the syntactic heads. For example, the choice of the preposition *on* in the sentence *I depend heavily on this evidence* is clearly determined by the head verb *depend*, even though it can be at a greater distance from the preposition as in *I depend almost exclusively and in nearly all the cases under discussion on this evidence.*

(b) *Parse information* enables access to syntactic information from the entire structure of a sentence, for example whether a noun phrase is modified by a relative clause, etc. Systems vary in whether they use parse information from a constituency parse or a dependency parse. *Chunk information* is a simpler variant, where the analysis component produces a chunk parse, identifying only the major phrase boundaries, such as such as noun phrases, verb phrases, etc.

3. *Semantic information* can be provided by outside resources such as dictionaries and semantic hierarchies. For example, nouns under an *organization* node in a semantic hierarchy will be more likely to be accompanied by the definite article (*the Peace Corps*). These outside resources can be manually compiled (such as WordNet, Miller [1995]), or can be the result of a distributional semantics approach that automatically clusters words in a corpus according to the contexts they occur in.

4. *Source information* such as the writer's word selection and the writer's native language can also be effective features for systems. Depending on the L1, for example, the confusion probabilities for prepositions are significantly different. Also, as noted earlier in Chapter 3, at least some of the errors that second language learners make are the result of negative transfer from their native languages. Therefore, it seems reasonable to expect systems to benefit from knowledge of the writer's L1, which would allow them to target specific errors and tailor their feedback to the background of the user.

5.2   TYPES OF TRAINING DATA

To date, most statistical approaches to grammatical error correction have used one of the following training paradigms:

1. training solely on examples of correct usage (such as in Han et al. [2006])

2. training on examples of correct usage and artificially generated errors [Rozovskaya and Roth, 2010c]

3. training on examples of correct usage and real learner errors [Dahlmeier and Ng, 2011a].

The choice of paradigm has largely been influenced by the availability of error-annotated corpora. Prior to 2009, there were very few publicly available learner corpora, let alone error-annotated data. To circumvent this problem, systems during this time were developed using the first paradigm, in which a statistical model was trained on only well-formed text and then used to predict the best preposition or article for a given context. The model's confidence in its prediction was compared to its confidence in the writer's choice, and if the difference was great enough, the writer's choice was flagged as an error. Note that in this paradigm there is no knowledge of general learner error patterns or errors that are made by native speakers of specific L1s. As interest increased in grammatical error correction, learner corpora became more readily available making it more tractable to develop systems that have knowledge of typical error patterns made by learners.

In the second paradigm, a classifier is trained on large amounts of well-formed text that is artificially populated with errors following some distribution. In the simplest case, the errors are introduced at random, for example, by changing one preposition to another. With at least some annotated learner data at hand, it is possible to produce a more realistic error distribution where the substitutions reflect real error tendencies among learners.

In the third paradigm (training on actual error-annotated data), a classifier is trained on examples of correct usage and examples of actual errors. We discuss these three paradigms in more detail in the following subsections.

5.2.1   TRAINING ON WELL-FORMED TEXT

Because early approaches to error detection and correction did not have access to large amounts of error-annotated data to train statistical models, systems were trained instead on millions of examples from available native corpora (typically news text) as in Gamon et al. [2008], Tetreault and Chodorow [2008a] and De Felice and Pulman [2009]. Feature sets usually consisted of n-grams around the article or preposition, POS sequences, syntactic and semantic features. Since the model only had knowledge of correct usage, an error was flagged if the system's prediction for a particular preposition/article context differed from the preposition or article the writer used by some margin.

In contrast to the sparseness of learner corpora, very large well-formed English corpora are widely available. State-of-the-art language models are often trained on resources such as the Gigaword corpus [Graff and Cieri, 2003] which contains nearly two billion words, and even larger web-based corpora have become available, for example the Google n-gram corpus [Brants and Franz, 2006] with more than a trillion tokens. Using these data sources one can, for example, estimate the probability of the preposition *on* occurring after *depend* based on bigram frequencies. If the preposition *to* is encountered after the verb *depend* in a learner's sentence, a quick comparison between the probability of *on* occurring instead of *to* in that position gives strong evidence for the correctness of *depend on* versus *depend to*. In one particular implementation of a Gigaword language model, the log probability of *depend on* is -27.29, while the log probability of *depend to* is only -33.28.

One of the main challenges for accurate grammatical error detection is to locate training materials that are appropriate for the type of writing that language learners need help with. Large publicly available corpora are often from the news domain or from encyclopedia text such as Wikipedia. The Gigaword corpus, for example, consists entirely of news data. While these data are plentiful, they also create a problem: the real-life writing of language learners does not look like newspaper text. For example, newspaper text is rarely written in the first person, but the content of an email message or a student essay will contain a number of first person pronouns.

Similarly, imperative sentences are typically used in email, but they are rarely found in newspapers. The same problem applies to questions, which occur relatively infrequently in news text, but are commonly found in learner writing. In the HOO shared tasks (discussed in Chapter 9), the focus was on correcting scientific writing, and text from the ACL anthology served as training material for many of the participating systems.

5.2.2   ARTIFICIAL ERRORS

In the absence of large-scale error data, one reasonable strategy is to artificially create an error corpus from a well-formed one. The simplest approach is to introduce errors randomly (for example random substitutions, insertions, and deletions of prepositions) in a large edited corpus, such as a collection of newswire or encyclopedia text. However, this strategy can prove challenging when used for machine learning experiments. Learners do not make random preposition errors; their errors of substitution, deletion, and insertion are distributed across prepositions in a particular way—often influenced by their native language. A fundamental rule of machine learning is that in order to achieve the best results, the distributions used for training should be as close as possible to the target (application) distributions. Consequently, the introduction of errors for an automated grammatical error detection system needs to stay as close as possible to the real types and distributions of errors made by language learners. Determining these distributions is itself a non-trivial goal. Even if error distributions can be reasonably approximated in an artificial error corpus, there are other differences that distinguish it from learner text. In a learner corpus, sentences often contain multiple errors of different kinds, but in the typical artificial error corpus, there is only a single error per sentence and that error is restricted to a predefined type.

There have been several strands of research that have shown at least some success employing artificially created error corpora. Izumi et al. [2003] was the first to evaluate a model trained on incorrect usage as well as artificial errors for the task of correcting several different error types, including prepositions. However, with limited training data, system performance was quite poor. Sjöbergh and Knutsson [2005] introduced two types of errors that learners of Swedish often make into a corpus of Swedish texts and then trained a transformation-based learner on the data. They also observed that the rule learner based on this artificial data set could outperform Swedish grammar checkers on recall, although precision did suffer. Brockett et al. [2006] explored the idea of treating automated error correction as a machine translation problem where the translation is from "English with mass/count noun errors" to "English without errors." The error data they used were created artificially from the error-free data. This work is discussed in more detail in Chapter 9. Lee and Seneff [2008] introduced verb form errors into a corpus to examine the parse patterns that these errors introduce when using a statistical parser. They then built and evaluated a system to detect these erroneous parse patterns. Use of artificially created error corpora was also proposed in Wagner et al. [2007, 2009] to train a classifier that detects grammatical errors. The focus in the earlier paper was on the best choice of features; the later paper extended the experiments to additional feature sets, evaluated the classifier on both artificial and real-life learner data, and used classifier voting. Foster and Andersen [2009] introduced their *GenERRate* tool that approximates real life errors. The input consisted of two data sets: a grammatical corpus and a list of real learner errors. The list of learner errors was specified along the four basic error mechanisms of substitution, deletion, insertion, and movement, with the possibility of further specifying parts of speech and/or lexical items. Additionally, frequency information about these errors and error templates was included in the error list. The algorithm then introduced errors into the corpus files along the lines of the pre-specified templates, and, if the information was provided, according to the frequency distribution. Initial experiments confirmed that this approach can be useful compared to using only a small- or medium-sized manually annotated corpus.

Perhaps the most in-depth study of using artificial error techniques for grammatical error correction is the work of Rozovskaya and Roth [2010c]. They evaluated four different paradigms of generating artificial errors in a training corpus of English from Wikipedia text. The task for evaluation was the article correction task. The four methods of error generation were: 1) replacing an article *x* by another article *y* at random at various rates; 2) changing the distribution of articles in the training data so it has the same distribution as found in an ESL text; 3) changing the distribution of articles in the training data so it has the same distribution as found in *corrected* ESL text; and 4) using distributions from the actual error patterns found in a corrected ESL set to create artificial errors. To illustrate this last paradigm, if 14% of the time *the* was incorrectly omitted in an annotated ESL corpus, then 14% of the occurrences of *the* would be deleted (changed to *null*) in the well-formed training corpus to generate artificial errors. The four paradigms for error generation were used to train classifiers, which were then evaluated on a corpus of ESL essays from Russian, Chinese, and Czech speakers. The authors found that training on the artificially created error data produced an improvement in performance over the standard paradigm of solely training on well-formed text. Rozovskaya and Roth [2010b] extend this work to preposition correction, where the introduction of artificial errors that mirror the distribution of L1-specific preposition confusions also greatly improves the classifier accuracy. As we shall see in Chapter 9, this also proved to be a winning strategy in the HOO shared tasks. Imamura et al. [2012] argue that these methods (in combination with additional techniques) could also be effective in the task of correcting particle errors in Japanese learner essays written by students whose native language was Chinese.

5.2.3 ERROR-ANNOTATED LEARNER CORPORA

Recently, error-annotated learner data have become more readily and publicly available allowing models to be trained both on examples of correct usage and on typical learner errors. Han et al. [2010] trained a classifier on the *Chungdahm English Learner Corpus*, a large corpus of student essays that were annotated by language tutors. The corpus used in the study totaled 861,481 essays. The corpus was only partially annotated because the tutors focused on a selection of error types at any given time in the curriculum, hence some of the "correct" examples in the corpus were actually errors that were not annotated by the tutor. Despite this source of noise in the training data, Han et al. [2010] found that a preposition error detection model trained on just under 1 million examples of correct and incorrect usage significantly outperformed a 4-million example model trained exclusively on well-formed text. Gamon [2010] and Dahlmeier and Ng [2011a] showed that combining models trained separately on examples of correct and incorrect usage could also improve the performance of a preposition error correction system.

The *lang-8.com* website,[1] which allows language learners to post content that is then edited and corrected by native speakers, has proven to be a valuable source of annotated learner errors in English, Japanese, and other languages. (See Section 8.3.3 for a more detailed description.) In addition to their work on Japanese error correction [Mizumoto et al., 2011], Tajiri et al. [2012] used the website to extract 2 million English verb phrases, along with corrections for 750,000 of them. Using this corpus, they were able to correct verb tense and aspect errors, though no comparison was made to the other training paradigms.

In the shared HOO and CoNLL tasks described in Chapter 9, error annotated texts from the ACL anthology and the *NUCLE* v2.3 corpus were used as training data respectively.

5.2.4   COMPARING TRAINING PARADIGMS

Izumi et al. [2003] presented the first attempt to compare the three training paradigms. Unfortunately, the sizes of their artificial learner corpus and annotated learner corpus were quite small, and thus performance across the three approaches was low. More recently, Cahill et al. [2013b] performed a comparison of the three paradigms over three different test corpora for the task of preposition error correction. Wikipedia texts and news texts served as well-formed training data. Artificial error corpora were derived from the distributions in two error-annotated corpora—Wikipedia (1 million corrected errors found in 7 million sentences in the revision history of Wikipedia articles) and content on the *lang-8.com* website. (The revisions derived from scraping the site will henceforth be called *lang-8*.) The latter data contained 53,000 errors found in 129,000 sentences. These two error-corrected corpora were also used directly to train models in a third series of experiments. For two of the test corpora, the artificial error model trained on *lang-8* error distributions significantly outperformed all other models. This work showed that models derived from different sources of error-corrected data outperformed models trained on solely well-formed text. It also showed that artificial error models can be competitive with models trained on real error corrections, most probably due to the large size that artificial error corpora can be scaled up to. Finally, models trained on the Wikipedia data tended to perform the best or nearly the best across the three test corpora, showing that Wikipedia revision history is a reliable and robust resource for error corrections.

[1]http://www.lang-8.com

5.3 METHODS

We now change our focus from the different types of data used for training to the different methods that distinguish the research. We first discuss two distinct groups of methods: classification and n-gram statistics-related methods.

5.3.1 CLASSIFICATION

A very common method for error correction is classification. The information gathered from the context of a preposition or article can be represented as a vector of features. At training time, a classifier learns which feature values (or, depending on the particular algorithm, which combination of features) influences the probability of a specific preposition/article choice. At runtime, the same features are extracted from the context of a candidate preposition/article, and the classifier predicts the best choice, or in the case of a calibrated classifier, the probability of each choice. We will present a number of classification approaches. The choice of classifier is often influenced by the number of features, size of the training set, speed and sometimes simply personal preference. An evaluation by Rozovskaya and Roth [2011] compared two classification approaches: Naïve Bayes and Averaged Perceptron, as well as two n-gram statistics methods: Language Models and n-gram frequencies, on different training sets and feature sets and found that the Averaged Perceptron outperformed the other three methods.

Minnen et al. [2000] built on an early classification-based approach for article correction of Knight and Chander [1994] that was motivated by the need for postediting of machine-translated documents. Where Knight and Chander [1994] had used a set of syntactically bracketed noun phrases for training, Minnen et al. [2000] employed an expanded feature set that included information derived from functional tags in the Penn Treebank, as well as from an external semantic hierarchy, and a lexicon of countability preferences of nouns. Lee [2004]'s system also derived syntactic features from a statistical Penn Treebank parser and semantic features from a large hand-crafted ontology (WordNet). His approach outperformed a re-implementation of Minnen et al. [2000] on the article prediction task on Penn Treebank data. He also observed that parser errors on text where articles had been omitted led to a degradation in his system's performance.

Nagata et al. [2005a,b, 2006a,b] focused on article errors made by Japanese learners of English. They presented a number of variations on a simple statistical model based on conditional probabilities of articles, given a variety of contextual features (head, multiple heads in the vicinity, etc.). They added hand-crafted heuristics to the system. Nagata et al. [2006c] explored the assumption that, within a single discourse, the mass/count status of a noun does not change. This added a useful additional source of evidence for the decision-making process.

Izumi et al. [2003, 2004c] targeted a wide range of omission, insertion, and substitution errors, including, but not limited to, articles and prepositions. Features used for the training of a maximum entropy classifier included lexical, morphological, and part-of-speech information from a context of two words to the left and right of the potential error location. In addition to error detection, each potential error was also classified as belonging to one of 45 [Izumi et al., 2003] or 13 [Izumi et al., 2004c] predefined error categories. Results were best for articles, the most frequent error type in the data. The classifier was trained on learner sentences with annotated errors, and the authors also experimented with including corrected sentences and sentences containing artificially generated errors. As mentioned earlier, one issue with these studies is that their system probably underperformed because its maximum entropy classifier was trained on a small error-annotated corpus.

Much of the early work using data-driven approaches adopted the tactic of training a statistical classifier on millions of examples of correct usage, and then flagging an error when the system's top choice for a given context is a much stronger candidate than the writer's choice. Han et al. [2004] used a maximum entropy classifier trained on 6 million noun phrases from the MetaMetrics *Lexile* corpus. Each potential article position was represented as a vector of lexical and part-of-speech features from the context of that position. The evaluation was conducted not only on four folds of the training data but also on 150 TOEFL essays. Han et al. [2006] further elaborated the evaluation scheme used in this work. Their system framework was adopted for ETS's preposition error detection system [Chodorow et al., 2007; Tetreault and Chodorow, 2008a, 2009] though with a feature set that is specific to preposition errors. This work was extended in Tetreault et al. [2010b] to include features based on phrase structure and dependency parses and extended in Cahill et al. [2013b] to accommodate models trained on artificial and real errors. De Felice and Pulman [2008] used similar features for their article and preposition error detection system and also included information from a named entity recognizer, WordNet, and grammatical relations extracted from a parser. Gamon et al. [2008] employed a decision tree as the main classifier in conjunction with a language model. This method was improved upon in Gamon [2010], which employed a meta-classifier trained on error-annotated data to combine scores from a maximum entropy classifier and a language model.

Dahlmeier and Ng [2011a] combined information from native text and from error-annotated learner data in an integrated learning algorithm called Alternating Structure Optimization (*ASO*) [Ando et al., 2005], as opposed to building different models and combining their output (as in Gamon [2010], for example). Targeted error types in their experiments were articles and prepositions. ASO leverages training information from a target task (learner error correction in this case), and from an auxiliary task (article/preposition selection on native data) in an integrated way by jointly minimizing error on the two tasks during training. They evaluated this approach on the *NUCLE* corpus against two baselines: training a classifier on only the native text or only the error-annotated learner data. Results showed that ASO achieved the best F-score compared to the baselines.

5.3.2 *N*-GRAM STATISTICS, LANGUAGE MODELS, AND WEB COUNTS

N-gram statistics and language models are other well-studied techniques to detect unusual word combinations and hence potential errors. If a sequence of words containing a particular article or preposition is much more probable than a sequence with an alternative article or preposition, then the less probable sequence is more likely to contain the wrong article or preposition. n-gram statistics can be extracted from data and calculated in different ways. The standard method is to employ a Language Model (LM). LMs are trained on large corpora. N-grams (typically up to 3 or 4 tokens in length) are counted in the corpus, and these counts are then used to compute the overall probability of any sequence of words. Unseen sequences of words are dealt with by "smoothing" algorithms that distribute a small amount of probability mass to unseen events in order to avoid zero-probabilities. Language models have been extremely successful in many areas of natural language processing, from speech recognition to machine translation (see Jurafsky and Martin [2008] for an excellent overview). A simpler technique for using n-gram statistics is to directly consult the observed counts of n-grams, either from a large n-gram frequency corpus such as the Google n-gram corpus or from consulting a web search engine by issuing an exact-match query for an n-gram and retrieving the estimated count of search results.

Language Model Approaches

Approaches using only language modeling for preposition and article prediction are rare and often use syntactic language models which contain parse information in addition to n-gram based information. Turner and Charniak [2007] utilized a language model based on parse trees from a statistical parser [Charniak, 2001] to determine the probability of a noun phrase with a null-article, a/an, or the in the context of the parse. Overall, the use of language models has increased in more recent systems; nearly half of the systems in the 2012 HOO shared task used some form of language model as a component, either as a post-filtering step to eliminate bad correction candidates or as a feature in the classification component. We will discuss these uses in greater detail in Chapter 9.

Lee and Seneff [2006] created a lattice with possible corrections for article, preposition, and verb form (aspect/mode and tense) errors. They first reduced their training data (transcribed speech from flight reservation dialogs) by eliminating articles, prepositions, and auxiliaries, and by stemming nouns and verbs, and then created a lattice by allowing articles, prepositions, and auxiliaries to be inserted between any two words, and nouns and verbs to be replaced by any possible inflectional variant. Every path through the lattice was scored by both an n-gram language model and a language model based on a probabilistic context-free grammar. The authors report that lattice scoring by the probabilistic context-free grammar outperformed scoring by the n-gram language model.

Gamon [2010] combined a large language model and a classification approach in a meta-learner which was trained on error-annotated data to weigh evidence from both methods optimally for error correction.

N-gram Approaches

Currently the largest corpus of n-grams is the Google n-gram corpus, which consists of billions of n-grams of lengths 1 through 5 scraped from the web. The advantage of using such data for error detection, or any other NLP task, is that it has the potential to alleviate the data sparseness problem confronting statistical models built from comparatively smaller data sets.

Bergsma et al. [2009] described a preposition selection method for well-formed text which uses the Google n-gram corpus. It takes all the n-grams from length 3 to 5 that overlap the target preposition, produces alternative n-grams by replacing the writer's preposition with other prepositions, and looks up the frequencies of these alternative n-grams in the corpus. Next, each preposition's "fit" for the context is ranked by the following: for each n-gram length, all the n-gram counts are summed, then the logarithm is taken. These three logs are then summed to produce a score for that preposition. Finally, the preposition with the highest score is selected. Using the logarithm lowers the contribution of the shorter length n-grams, which are likely to have very large counts and lack the necessary context. This method showed an accuracy of 71% on well-formed text, but no experiments were conducted on learner text. Elghafari et al. [2010] showed that performance on well-formed text could be further improved by using a 7-gram window as well as a back-off model.

While the Google n-gram corpus has proven to be useful for several NLP tasks, it remains an open question how best to use it for detecting and correcting learners' errors. The potential drawback of this method is that it can be brittle if the context around the target error also contains errors. In these situations there will be very little n-gram support. As a result, it is common that systems combine n-gram approaches with other approaches. For example, Tetreault and Chodorow [2008a] incorporated the top three prepositions predicted from using the Google n-gram corpus as additional features in their maximum entropy model, although this inclusion only improved performance marginally.

5.3.3   WEB-BASED METHODS

Web-based methods for article error detection [Yi et al., 2008] and preposition error detection [Boyd and Meurers, 2011; Elghafari et al., 2010; Hermet and Désilets, 2009; Hermet et al., 2008; Tetreault and Chodorow, 2009] are an alternative to the use of a language model or an n-gram corpus. These methods are based on the use of a commercial web search engine. The count of a particular n-gram on the web is approximated by the search engine's estimate of total returned search results when the n-gram is entered as a search query. In order to avoid spurious matches, the n-gram is entered as an "exact match" query, i.e., it is enclosed in double quotes.

One of the first uses of the web for checking spelling and idioms was the *Penguin* system developed by Fallman [2002]. In *Penguin*, the user enters a string, such as a word or idiomatic expression, and the system accesses a search engine and displays the number of hits and examples for that string, as well as for its alternatives. The actual error checking is done by the user as the system only provides information and does not make any diagnostic suggestions. One advantage of a web-based system such as this is that it is dynamic: As language changes, the web search hits will also change and reflect the state of language use better than static tables or rules.

Yi et al. [2008] described a web-based proofreading system for article and collocation errors. The system works by first parsing ELL sentences and identifying checkpoints that describe the context around the article or collocation. Given the checkpoints, queries are generated to find appropriate examples from the web. In the case of articles, three queries are generated, corresponding to the context with the article position filled by *a/an, the*, and *null*. This method goes beyond simply comparing the counts returned from the three queries. First, each count is multiplied by the length (number of words) of the query to generate a weighted count. This helps compensate for long queries since they will have smaller web counts than short queries. Next, two thresholds are used to flag an error. First, if the weighted count is too low, there is not enough "support" from the web to determine if an error exists, so these cases are skipped. Then, the weighted count for the writer's article is compared to the top weighted count. If this ratio is not larger than another threshold, it indicates that the writer's choice is not strong enough and thus an error is flagged. When the system was evaluated on different threshold settings, the best setting performed at 40.7% recall and 62.5% precision, which is not too far below the performance of classifier-based systems.

Hermet et al. [2008] employed a similar algorithm for the correction of preposition errors by writers learning French. In their procedure, for each preposition in a sentence, the words surrounding the target preposition are pruned and generalized. Second, a list of alternative prepositions that are commonly confused with the writer's preposition is generated. Third, a new phrase is created with the original replaced by each of the alternative prepositions. These new phrases, and the original, are sent to a web search query engine and the web counts are recorded. The alternative preposition with the highest count is selected as the correction. The system was evaluated on 133 sentences from French language learners. Each sentence contained at least one preposition error. The system successfully corrected 69.9% of the prepositions, outperforming the majority preposition baseline (24.8%) and a leading French grammar checker (3.1%). The authors also noted that the size of the reference corpus has a significant effect on performance. If instead of the web, *n*-grams are used that occur at least 40 times on the French web, then performance drops to 59.4%. Using a thousandth of the French web further lowered performance to 30.8%.

Tetreault and Chodorow [2009] proposed a novel web-based method for discovering common L1 transfer errors. The procedure uses the "region" search found in both the Google and the Yahoo search APIs to compare the distribution of a target English construction on webpages in the United States (or another predominantly English-speaking country) to the distribution of the same English construction on webpages in a predominantly non-English speaking country. If the distributions of the English construction differ markedly between the two regions, then this indicates that the construction may be problematic for native speakers of that L1. For example, using a search of webpages in the U.S. *depends on* is used 345 times more often than *depends of*, but a search of English webpages in France shows that *depends on* occurs 66 times more often. Since this is considerably less than the U.S. ratio, the construction would be flagged as problematic. They demonstrated that this methodology can "discover" errors that have been described in the ELL literature.

Table 5.1: Region Counts Example for "depends *preposition*"

However, web methods are not without their problems. Kilgarriff [2007] noted several concerns:

1. Commercial search engines do not tag for part-of-speech and do not lemmatize.

2. Search syntax is often limited (e.g., wild cards are not always available).

3. There are constraints on the number of queries per day, and hits per query. This seriously limits running experiments or deploying an operational system that requires thousands or millions of queries.

4. Search counts are for pages, not for instances.

5. Different search engines exhibit different behaviors. For example, web counts from the Google and Bing search engines on the same string often differ by several orders of magnitude and ratios are often not comparable.

An issue with web methods particular to their use for ELL error detection and correction is how best to construct queries. Second language writing often contains many errors in a single sentence, so the context around a target error is itself likely to contain one or more errors of various types. If the context is used as part of the query, then it is likely to return few, if any, hits due to these other adjacent errors. To address this data noise problem, Hermet et al. [2008] divide the sentence around the target preposition and parse each part individually, only extracting the main noun and verb phrases.

Another issue with using web counts, as we have mentioned, is that different search engines exhibit different behaviors, and to further complicate matters, web counts returned from a query can actually vary from day to day, or even hour to hour [Tetreault and Chodorow, 2009].

5.4 TWO END-TO-END SYSTEMS: *CRITERION* AND MSR *ESL ASSISTANT*

Some of the technologies discussed in the previous section are used in at least two larger-scale systems which we will describe in some detail. The first system has been developed by Educational

Testing Service [Burstein et al., 2004] as part of the *Criterion*^{SM} *Online Writing Evaluation Service*. Article error detection became part of *Criterion* in 2005, and preposition error detection was added in 2008. The second system is the Microsoft Research *ESL Assistant* [Gamon et al., 2008], which was made public as a prototype web service from June of 2008 until April 2010. Both systems provide a range of grammatical error detection and correction, but we will only focus on preposition errors for illustration.

Criterion uses maximum entropy classifiers for both article and preposition error detection and correction. The classifiers are trained on part-of-speech tagged input from well-formed text. For articles, the training consists of 6 million usage contexts extracted from *The San Jose Mercury News* and the MetaMetrics *Lexile* corpus of 11th and 12th grade material, and for prepositions, it consists of 7 million contexts covering 34 of the most common prepositions. The part-of-speech tags are used by a heuristic chunker to identify noun phrase and prepositional phrase boundaries as sites where articles and prepositions are present or could potentially be present. Each potential position of an article or preposition is represented as a vector of features, including the features in Table 5.2, with example values for the input string *We sat at the sunshine*. In addition to the features shown, a special set of combination features that simultaneously encode both the left and right contexts is used by the system. To reduce potential false positives, *Criterion* employs some post-processing filters that apply after the classifier has cast its vote. These filters are heuristic in nature and include the following: (1) If the classifier predicts an antonym of the writer's preposition, the prediction is blocked in order to avoid reversal of meaning by, for example, suggesting *the package was shipped from X* when the original sentence is *the package was shipped to X*. (2) A prepositional phrase with the preposition *for* and a human object is not flagged as an error since these benefactive phrases can occur freely in all kinds of contexts. (3) Extraneous use errors are covered by rules that deal with repeated prepositions, misuse of quantifiers (*some of people*), and other cases where the preposition should be deleted. Figure 5.1 shows a screenshot of *Criterion*'s user interface.

MSR *ESL Assistant* uses two maximum entropy classifiers each for preposition and article error detection. One classifier predicts whether an article/preposition is likely to be present in a given context (*presence classifier*), and the second predicts the particular choice of article/preposition given the context (*choice classifier*). As in *Criterion*, feature vectors are extracted from the training data. The features in *ESL Assistant* consist of part-of-speech tags and word-based features from a context of six tokens to the right and left, as listed in Table 5.3.

The training data for *ESL Assistant* consist of text from six domains: Encarta encyclopedia text, Reuters newswire, transcripts of UN sessions, transcripts of EU sessions, and general web-scraped content. The number of feature vectors for training is similar to *Criterion* at 16.5 million. The system covers 12 prepositions. In addition to the classifiers, *ESL Assistant* also uses a large language model trained on the Gigaword corpus (Linguistic Data Consortium 2003) as additional evidence.

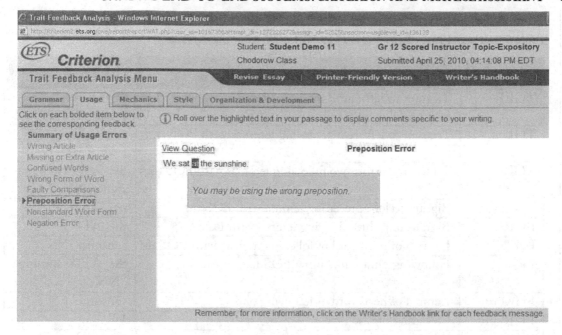

Figure 5.1: Screenshot of the *Criterion* interface.

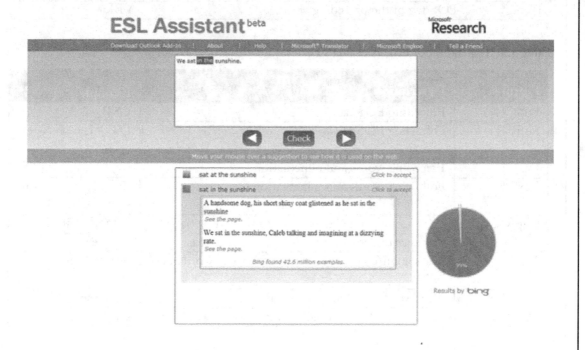

Figure 5.2: Screenshot of the MSR's *ESL-Assistant* interface.

Table 5.2: Partial List of *Criterion's* Features for *We sat at the sunshine*

Feature	Description	Example
TGLR	Trigram to left and right: preceding lemma with POS tag and following lemma with POS tag	sit_VBD-1+the_ATI+1
TGL	Trigram to left: two preceding lemmas with POS tags	we_PRP-2+sit_VBD-1
TGR	Trigram to right: two following lemmas with POS tags	the_ATI+1+ sunshine _NN+2
BGL	Bigram to left: preceding lemma with POS tag	sit_VBD-1
BGR	Bigram to right: following lemma with POS tag	the_ATI+1
FH	Lemma of headword of following phrase with POS tag	sunshine_NN
FP	Following phrase including POS tags	the_ATI+ sunshine _NN
FHword	Lemma of headword of following phrase	sunshine
PHR_pre	Preceding phrase type	VP
PV	Preceding verb lemma with POS tag	sit_VBD
FHtag	POS tag of headword of the following phrase	NN
PVtag	POS tag of the preceding verb	VBD

Table 5.3: Partial List of ESL Assistant's Features for *We sat at the sunshine*

Feature	Description	Example
PoSCL	Preceding POS tags	PNP_-2, VP_-1
PoSCR	Following POS tags	DT_+1, NN_+2, ._+3
LexCL	Preceding words and punctuation	we_-2, sat_-1
LexCR	Following words and punctuation	the_+1, sunshine_+2, ._+3
CapR/CapL	Presence of capitalized tokens to the left or right	< none available>
AcrR/AcrL	Presence of acronyms (tokens in all upper case)	< none available>
MN	Mass noun/count noun status of the headword of the NP	massNoun
HeadNP	Headword of the following NP	sunshine
HeadVP	Headword of the preceding VP	sat

In the 2010 version of *ESL Assistant* [Gamon, 2010], all the available scores from the classifiers and the language model are collected and passed on to a decision tree meta-classifier that combines them for a final judgment. The meta-classifier is trained on error-annotated data (*Cambridge Learners Corpus*). For each potential preposition/article location, it uses the language model scores, the presence classifier's probability, the choice classifier's probability, the type of correction (deletion, insertion, or substitution), the writer's original word, and the system's suggested correction as input features. It then uses these features to predict if the suggested correction is valid or not, based on the evidence it has seen during training. For more details of this approach and its benefits over a classifier or language model alone, see Gamon [2010].

In addition to error detection and correction, *ESL Assistant* also offers examples of both the original usage and the suggested correction based on a web search, with a visualization of how frequently the original usage is found on the web compared to the suggested usage. The screenshot in Figure 5.2 illustrates this functionality, which mimics the behavior of many learners who use multiple queries to a web search engine to determine the correct word choice.

5.5 SUMMARY

Research on the detection and correction of article and preposition errors has formed the bulk of the work in the NLP error correction community over the last ten years. This is largely due to the fact that these errors are some of the most common and most challenging for all language learners, and are also two kinds of errors for which statistical methods provide a more favorable approach than using hand-crafted rules.

In this chapter we have discussed three interacting directions of research that the field has taken to design and improve data-driven models for article and preposition correction. The focus has been on the types of features used for modeling (lexical, syntactic, semantic, and information on the learner's L1), the nature and size of the training data (well-formed, error-annotated learner data, data with artificially created errors), and the kinds of statistical models used (classifiers, language models, syntactic language models). Many of these findings have influenced the treatment of other error types, as we shall see in Chapter 7 as well as the methods used in the recent error correction shared tasks (Chapter 9).

CHAPTER 6

Collocation Errors

We know that words do not combine randomly in natural language, as their distributions are governed by both syntax and semantics. But beyond grammar and meaning, words also show tendencies or preferences in the ways they combine. As we noted in Chapter 3, native speakers of English know that the noun phrase *powerful computer* is preferred over *strong computer*, even though both are grammatically and semantically well formed. Examples of such arbitrary, conventional usage appear in many different syntactic constructions, including adjective + noun (*stiff breeze* instead of *rigid breeze*), verb + noun (*hold an election* instead of *make an election*; *kick the bucket* (in the *die* sense) instead of *hit the bucket*), noun + noun or noun + of + noun (*movie theater* instead of *film theater*; *swarm of bees* instead of *crowd of bees*), and adverb + verb (*thoroughly amuse* instead of *completely amuse*).[1] Preferred word combinations such as these were first termed "collocations" by Firth [1957]. In the Firthian approach, the context of a word's usage is seen as crucially important in determining the word's meaning. This view underlies Firth's now-famous dictum that "you shall know a word by the company it keeps."

6.1 DEFINING COLLOCATIONS

Linguists have tried to define exactly what a collocation is. One proposed criterion is non-compositionality, which states that the meaning of the collocation is not entirely a function of its parts. Non-compositionality can be seen most clearly in idioms such as *to kick the bucket*, where the idiomatic meaning of the whole (i.e., *to die*) seems unrelated to the parts *kick* or *bucket*. However, many collocations are indeed compositional (e.g., *powerful computer*). Another proposed criterion is non-modifiability. Many collocations cannot be freely modified without fundamentally altering their meaning. For example, *to kick a plastic bucket* has only the literal meaning, not the idiomatic one. But, once again, many collocations are modifiable without a change in meaning (e.g., *powerful new computer*). Another property, non-substitutability, seems to be characteristic of almost all collocations. It refers to the inability to substitute a near synonym for part of a collocation, as shown in our earlier examples, such as *a powerful/strong computer*. The debate continues over the proper definition of a collocation, as different people define it in different ways. For example, some include idioms and others do not. From a computational perspective, the properties of non-compositionality, non-modifiability, and non-substitutability suggest that collocations will differ distributionally from their non-collocational counterparts. As we will see later, distributional

---

[1]Please see *The BBI Dictionary of Combinatory English Words* [Benson et al., 1997] for a list of patterns in which collocations appear.

differences form the basis of computational approaches to detecting and correcting collocation errors. Because these approaches do not make direct use of meaning, they differ fundamentally from the lexicographic tradition [Mel'čuk, 1996; Ramos et al., 2010], which views a collocation as a syntactic construction comprised of a base word and a collocate whose meaning depends upon that of the base (e.g., *hold* in *hold an election*) or whose selection seems to depend arbitrarily on the base word (e.g., *powerful* in *powerful computer*).

6.2   MEASURING THE STRENGTH OF ASSOCIATION BETWEEN WORDS

Much of the NLP literature on collocations is related to studies of indexing and technical terminology. Justeson and Katz [1995] used *n*-gram frequencies to identify technical terms in text. Of course, the most frequently occurring bigrams and trigrams are of little interest as terms or as collocations because they consist primarily of common function words, such as *in the*, or *is one of*. Justeson and Katz filtered out all sequences except for bigrams and trigrams consisting of contiguous nouns and adjectives, such as A+N, N+N, A+A+N, A+N+N, or nouns followed by preposition + noun, such as N+of+N. After sorting by frequency, this simple method yielded a large number of noun phrases that were topically relevant to the documents of their corpus (e.g., *linear function*, *degrees of freedom*).

Mathematical and statistical approaches to identifying collocations use formulas to measure the strength of association between words. The words within a collocation are expected to be more strongly associated than non-collocation items. So, if all bigrams in a corpus are extracted, measured for associative strength, and then ranked on the basis of the measure, the bigrams near the top of the ranking should be better examples of collocations than those near the bottom.[2] Judging which examples are good and which are bad is sometimes left to the intuition of the researcher, and sometimes it is based on whether the collocation is found in an electronic dictionary or database such as WordNet.

There is certainly no shortage of ways to measure associative strength.[3] Excellent descriptions of several statistical tests and mathematical measures for collocation can be found in Manning and Schütze [1999]. Pecina [2005] presents the formulas for 84 such measures, which he evaluated in his study of collocations in Czech. He divides them into several classes, including statistical tests of independence [Church and Hanks, 1990; Dunning, 1993], information-theoretic indices [Church et al., 1991], and measures of contextual entropy [Shimohata et al., 1997]. Perhaps the most commonly used of these measures are the chi-square tests and pointwise mutual information.

Chi-Square Statistical Tests. A typical strategy is to compute a measure of associative strength between the words of the collocation and compare the measure to the value that would

---

[2]See Evert [2004] for a comprehensive treatment of these methods and procedures.

[3]Ted Petersen's Ngram Statistics Package (http://www.d.umn.edu/~tpederse/nsp.html) implements many standard tests of association for finding word and character *n*-grams in large corpora.

be expected if the words co-occurred by chance alone. A statistical test comparing the observed data to a model of chance co-occurrence can be based on the t, z, or chi-square distributions (see Chapter 5 in Manning and Schütze [1999]). For example, consider a bigram consisting of the two words, w_1 and w_2. The process begins with the construction of a contingency table (see Table 6.1) representing the unigram and bigram frequencies of w_1 and w_2 in a corpus. The cell for $w_1 w_2$ contains the bigram frequency. The marginal totals for w_1 and w_2 are their unigram frequencies. The labels $\neg w_1$ and $\neg w_2$ represent the absence of w_1 and w_2, respectively, and their marginal totals are equal to the total frequency (N) of all bigrams in the corpus minus the unigram frequency of each word. In the hypothetical example shown in the table, the total frequency of all bigrams in the corpus is 500, w_1 occurs 50 times, w_2 occurs 25 times, and the bigram $w_1 w_2$ occurs 20 times.

Table 6.1: Observed Frequencies for Bigram $w_1 w_2$

From these observed frequencies, the maximum likelihood estimates of the unigram and bigram probabilities are $P(w_1) = 50/500 = 0.10$; $P(w_2) = 25/500 = 0.05$; $P(w_1 w_2) = 20/500 = 0.04$. What would we have expected the table frequencies to be if w_1 and w_2 were independent of each other? Two events, A and B, are independent if $P(A \cap B) = P(A) * P(B)$, so we would have expected the probability of the bigram $w_1 w_2$ to be equal to $P(w_1) * P(w_2) = 50/500 * 25/500 = 0.005$, and, therefore, the expected frequency of the bigram to be $0.005 * 500 = 2.5$. The contingency table of expected frequencies is shown in Table 6.2.

Table 6.2: Expected Frequencies for the Bigram $w_1 w_2$

The strength of association between w_1 and w_2 can be measured by computing the difference between the observed and the expected tables. Pearson's chi-square test of independence does just that. If O_{ij} represents the *observed* frequency in the cell in row i and column j, and if E_{ij} represents the *expected* frequency in the cell in row i and column j, then:

$$\chi^2 = \sum_{i,j} \frac{(O_{ij} - E_{ij})^2}{E_{ij}}$$

For our example:

$$\chi^2 = \frac{(20 - 2.5)^2}{2.5} + \frac{(5 - 22.5)^2}{22.5} + \frac{(30 - 47.5)^2}{47.5} + \frac{(445 - 427.5)^2}{427.5} = 143.27$$

If the frequencies are large, then χ^2 will be distributed as the chi-square statistic with one degree of freedom (df). (There is only one df here because, when the marginal totals are fixed, only one cell in the table is free to vary, as all the others are constrained by the requirement that they add up to the marginal totals.) The chi-square distribution gives us the probability that the difference between the observed and expected frequencies is due to chance, i.e., the probability that w_1 and w_2 are independent. With $df = 1$, the probability of getting a value of χ^2 as large as the value we obtained, 143.27, is much less than 0.001, so we can conclude that w_1 and w_2 are non-independent, i.e., they are associated. One problem with χ^2 is that it is not a good approximation of chi-square when the expected frequency in any of the cells is small, for example, less than 5. This is the case for one cell in our example.

Dunning [1993] has shown that a better approximation to chi-square, especially with low expected frequencies, is the Log Likelihood Ratio test, which is based on the formula:

$$G^2 = 2 \sum_{i,j} O_{ij} \ln \left(\frac{O_{ij}}{E_{ij}} \right)$$

For our example:

$$G^2 = 2(20 \ln \left(\frac{20}{2.5} \right) + 5 \ln \left(\frac{5}{22.5} \right) + 30 \ln \left(\frac{30}{47.5} \right) + 445 \ln \left(\frac{445}{427.5} \right)) = 33.12$$

As the frequencies get larger (i.e., asymptotically), this measure is also distributed as chi-square, and, although its value in this example is smaller than the χ^2 we calculated earlier for the same data, it too indicates that the difference between the observed and expected frequencies is very unlikely to be the result of chance (the probability of it being so is also less than 0.001). The log likelihood ratio test is more robust than Pearson's chi-square for small frequencies, but neither test should be used when an expected frequency is less than 1. As an alternative, Pedersen [1996] presents the case for using Fisher's Exact Test, especially when dealing with very small counts.

Pointwise Mutual Information. Many measures of association cannot be used for statistical tests of independence, but they can be used for the purpose of ranking candidate collocations. Manning and Schütze [1999] (p. 183) describe pointwise mutual information as an information theoretic measure of "the reduction of uncertainty about the occurrence of one word when we are told about the occurrence of the other." The formula is:

$$I(w_1, w_2) = \log_2 \left(\frac{P(w_1 \, w_2)}{P(w_1) \, P(w_2)} \right)$$

For our example:

$$I(w_1, w_2) = \log_2 \left(\frac{0.04}{0.10 * 0.05} \right) = \log_2 (8.0) = 3.0$$

This represents a reduction of uncertainty of 3 bits. By contrast, if two words are independent, then their joint probability will equal the product of their individual probabilities, so the ratio in the above equation will be 1, and the log of the ratio will be 0. Larger values of pointwise mutual information indicate a greater strength of association; smaller values correspond to weaker association. Many researchers have been critical of the performance of this measure for finding good collocations. Manning and Schütze [1999] point out that the measure is especially adversely affected by sparseness of data. In particular, for non-independent bigrams, the pointwise mutual information value actually gets larger as the bigram frequency gets smaller. Despite these problems, it continues to be popular.

Studies that have compared the performance of word association measures have often yielded inconsistent or contradictory results [Evert and Krenn, 2001; Inkpen and Hirst, 2002; Krenn and Evert, 2001]. Evert and Krenn [2005] (p. 450) argued that, for statistical measures of association:

> The results of an evaluation experiment cannot easily be generalized to a different setting. Consequently, such experiments have to be carried out under conditions that are as similar as possible to the intended use of the measures.

Sometimes a theoretically superior measure performs less well than a competitor when put to an actual corpus-based test, as when Evert [2004] found that X^2 outperformed G^2 in ranking German adjective-noun combinations, or when Pecina [2005] found pointwise mutual information to be the single best of the 84 measures that he tested in his study of Czech collocations.

Not all approaches measure word association based on the independence assumption. Bouma [2010] describes the use of aggregate Markov Models (AMMs) to generate expected probabilities of word co-occurrence that can be used in a non-independence version of the mutual information formula. In AMMs, bigram probability is modeled using hidden class variables that incorporate more information than a unigram model but less information than a full bigram model. The number of classes determines the amount of dependency between words. AMMs can capture syntactic, lexical, semantic, and pragmatic dependencies. Bouma found superior performance for AMMs compared to standard PMI for the task of ranking the quality of German adjective-noun collocations. However, this was not the case for German PP-verb collocations.

A Rank-Based Measure. Deane [2005]'s rank ratio is a measure of associative strength based on frequency rank rather than on frequency or probability. It avoids several well-known problems that face other measures.

1. The t, z, and chi-square statistical tests and the information-theoretic measures compare a bigram to a default model of statistical independence, but words are clearly not independent as their distributions reflect syntactic and semantic constraints of language.

2. The statistical tests also assume that words are normally distributed, but their distributions are known to be highly skewed.

3. Collocations are not restricted to bigrams, but it is not clear how to extend many of the association measures to sequences of three or more words.

The rank ratio avoids these problems by providing a non-parametric measure which does not assume independence and which can be used to compare strength of association across sequences of different lengths.

To calculate the rank ratio, start with the frequencies of all the contexts (word sequences up to some maximum length) in which a particular target word appears. For example, suppose we look at all of the contexts of the word *east*, such as *east end*, *toward the east*, *east side*, etc. Rank all of these sequences from highest to lowest in terms of their frequencies in the corpus. For the sake of this example, suppose that *east side* is the second highest in frequency ($rank = 2$). This is a kind of conditional rank, conditioned in the sense that the ranks are based on frequencies of all the contexts that contain *east*. Next, look at the frequencies of all of the contexts that contained *east*, but this time without regard to the word that occupies the position which *east* had filled. In other words, find the frequencies of ** end*, *toward the **, ** side*, etc., where * is a wildcard. Let's suppose that ** side* is the fourth highest in frequency ($rank = 4$) for these * contexts. We might think of this as an *unconditional rank* as it does not depend on the presence of *east*. The rank ratio is equal to the unconditional rank divided by the conditional rank, in this case, $4/2 = 2$. It is a nonparametric measure of how salient the context is with the word *east* compared to the context's salience without the word *east*. A rank ratio can also be calculated for *east side*, that is, for the context *east* given the target word *side*. Then, to combine these measures, the mutual rank ratio of the sequence *east side* is defined as the geometric mean of its component rank ratios. Deane [2005] compared the mutual rank ratio to seven other association measures and showed it to be superior in finding phrasal terms (multi-word expressions listed in WordNet) in a large text corpus.

6.3 SYSTEMS FOR DETECTING AND CORRECTING COLLOCATION ERRORS

The problem of detecting collocation errors is similar in many ways to that of detecting article or preposition errors using a training corpus of only well-formed text. The strategy in each case is to compare the writer's word choice to alternative choices, and if one or more alternatives provide a much better fit to the context, then the writer's word is flagged as an error and the alternatives are suggested as corrections. In the case of article errors, there are just two alternatives to consider, and even for prepositions, the alternatives constitute a relatively small, fixed set. But collocation errors differ inasmuch as their alternatives involve substitutions from potentially very large sets of open class words, i.e., nouns, verbs, adjectives, and adverbs. (In fact, what we have been referring to as collocations are sometimes called "lexical collocations" to distinguish them from "grammatical collocations," which involve function words such as articles and prepositions.)

To constrain these substitution sets, only words with meanings similar to the writer's word are used. A general approach then might consist of four steps:

1. target syntactic constructions of a particular type or types, such as verb+noun;

2. for each example of the construction in the writer's text, create a set of alternatives by substituting words with similar meaning (strong → powerful in *a _____ computer*);

3. measure the strength of association in the writer's phrase and in each generated alternative phrase;

4. flag the writer's phrase if the association measure is lower (compared to some threshold amount) than one or more of the alternatives and suggest the higher-ranking alternatives as corrections.

Before we review the research literature, it is worth noting that the same challenges that are faced in evaluating systems for other kinds of usage errors are encountered in evaluating collocation error detection and correction systems. Chief among these is the relative unavailability of shared test corpora. In fact, to the best of our knowledge, none of the collocation systems described below were tested on the same corpus. There are hopeful signs that this situation will improve. Collocation errors were included in the HOO 2011 shared task, although there were few of them, and they were not evaluated separately from other types of errors in an "Other" category.

Lin [1999]'s work on finding non-compositional phrases in text illustrates steps (1) and (2). He used a dependency parser to find verb+object, adjective+noun, and noun+noun constructions in a corpus of 125 million words of newspaper text, and then used his corpus-based thesaurus [Lin, 1998] to find words of similar meaning in order to generate alternative phrases. Lin considered a phrase to be non-compositional, and therefore a good candidate for a collocation, if its pointwise mutual information value was significantly greater than the values of all the alternative phrases. The goal of this work was not to find collocation errors in non-native writing, so we have no measure of how the system would perform in such a task.

In recent years, online systems have been developed (a) to show English language learners the collocations that appear on the webpages they are browsing [Wible et al., 2006], (b) to support e-learning by providing web-based examples of various collocation types, and (c) to offer suggestions to learners about how a phrase might best be re-worded. An instance of the latter is "Just The Word",[4] developed by Sharp Laboratories of Europe. The user types a phrase into a textbox and is shown a bar graph of the collocational strength of the phrase, as measured by the value of its *t* statistic [Church and Hanks, 1990], along with the strengths of other phrases with similar meaning. A red bar indicates that a phrase is bad while green means that it is good. This is clearly close to an error detection and correction system although it does not extract the phrases automatically from text but instead requires them to be entered by the user.

---

[4]http://www.just-the-word.com/

An early system that did extract collocation errors in learner text was that of Shei and Pain [2000]. It located verb+noun and adverb+adjective constructions and looked them up in a reference database to see whether they were acceptable forms. If not found, they were looked up in an ESL error database and marked as errors if they were listed in the database. A thesaurus was used to generate alternative phrases, and if an alternative was found in the reference database, it was given as a suggestion. A manually constructed paraphrase dictionary was also consulted. Because this system seems to have relied on at least some manually constructed resources, such as an error database and a paraphrase dictionary, it is not clear how much effort would be required to extend it to other constructions and other error types.

Wible et al. [2003] developed a system to detect collocation errors in verb+noun constructions, but it was limited to nine nouns and used manually constructed sets of verbs that were known to combine with the nouns to form collocation errors. The system's precision was quite high at 95%, but with so much reliance on handcrafted resources, it would likely be difficult and costly to extend its coverage to more nouns and verbs, and to more types of collocations.

Futagi et al. [2008] used the rank ratio (RR) measure [Deane, 2005] based on frequencies from a corpus of more than one billion words consisting of literary and scientific journal articles and of elementary to post-graduate level texts. To generate alternatives, synonyms were taken from WordNet and Roget's Thesaurus. The researchers targeted six kinds of collocations, which were extracted from 300 randomly selected TOEFL essays. In all, there were 1,260 collocation strings that were evaluated by two human raters as *acceptable* or *error*. Rater 1 judged 17.6% of the collocations to be errors, and Rater 2, 15.1%. The level of inter-rater agreement was high at 88%. The system's classification of a collocation proceeded as follows: If the collocation had an RR value greater than an empirically set threshold and none of its alternative phrases had a much greater RR, then the collocation was labeled *acceptable*. It was labeled *error* if its RR was less than the threshold or if it was not found in the corpus or if an alternative phrase had a much greater RR. In the latter case, the alternative was suggested as a correction. The system's level of agreement with Rater 1 on the binary *acceptable versus error* judgment was 79%, and with Rater 2, 77%. When the results were analyzed in terms of precision and recall, there was a very clear difference between the system's performance on collocations that one or both of the raters considered acceptable and those that they did not. The F-score for acceptable collocations was 91%, but for error collocations it was only 34%. This mirrored a difference in agreement between the human raters for acceptable (average agreement = 90%) and error (average agreement = 60%) collocations. In other words, in both the human and human-system comparisons, agreement was higher for acceptable judgments than for error judgments. Finally, an analysis of the system's misclassifications revealed that a large proportion were due to data sparseness, suggesting that significant improvements could be made by using a larger training corpus.

Östling and Knutsson [2009] examined collocation errors in Swedish. They used a synonym dictionary, a word similarity measure based on random indexing, mutual information, and log-likelihood to find and rank candidate corrections for 30 verb-noun and 30 adjective-noun miscollocations that were artificially generated. A combination of their four word association measures produced the best results, 57% acceptable corrections.

Liu et al. [2009] explored the value of "collocation clusters" in generating corrections for collocation errors. Consider the verb-noun collocation error *reach a purpose*. Their system generates a cluster by finding verbs that collocate with the noun *purpose* and nouns that collocate with the verb *reach*. This produces a cluster with verbs such as *fulfill*, *achieve*, and *realize*, and with nouns such as *dream*, *ambition*, and *goal*. Not every verb in the cluster appears in collocations with every noun, so the verbs can be ranked based on the number of collocates that they share with *reach*. The highest ranking verbs that also have *purpose* as a collocate (*fulfill* and *achieve*) can then be offered as suggested corrections. The authors found that ranking this process of ranking the verbs by the number of collocates that they share with the error verb performed better than using mutual information alone, and that a model that combined the ranking with mutual information and a semantic similarity measure derived from WordNet performed better than any single feature. Wu et al. [2010] extracted verb + noun collocations from parsed sentences and generated features from the head noun and from unigrams and bigrams in the context around the collocation. With these features, they trained a maximum entropy classifier to predict the verb. Given a test sentence with the verb removed, their system returns a ranked list of suggestions. The researchers were able to show the relative value of using only the head noun, only the context, or both the head and the context in the classifier.

To date, perhaps the best-performing system for collocation error detection and correction is that of Chang et al. [2008], which targeted English verb+noun collocation errors produced by Chinese native speakers. In the first phase, verb+noun candidate collocations were extracted from the writer's text. Next, these were looked up in a collocation list created by Jian et al. [2004], who used the log-likelihood measure and a high threshold value to produce a list of more than 630,000 different collocations from the *British National Corpus* (*BNC*).[5] If the candidate collocation was found in the list, then it was considered acceptable; otherwise, it was marked as an error. An earlier study by Liu [2002] had shown that a large proportion of collocation errors made by native Chinese speakers are related to first language interference (for example, as a result of direct translation from Chinese to English). Therefore, in order to generate corrections, Chang, et al. used English-Chinese word lists that were derived from bilingual dictionaries and from a word-aligned bilingual English-Chinese parallel corpus. For example, the Chinese word for *eat* sometimes corresponds to the English *eat* and sometimes to other English words, such as *take* (as in *take the pill*). As a result, *eat* and *take* were placed in the same "synonym set" because both corresponded to Chinese *eat* in at least some context. When *eat the medicine* was encountered in non-native text, the alternative phrase *take the medicine* was generated as a candidate correction, which was then checked against the list of collocations that had been extracted from the *BNC* to filter out any that might be unacceptable. The system was tested on 200 correct verb-noun collocations from a bilingual text corpus and 226 incorrect verb-noun collocations from student writing.

[5]http://www.natcorp.ox.ac.uk/

The overall accuracy in the detection task was an impressive 98% precision and 91% recall. The quality of the suggested corrections was measured in terms of mean reciprocal rank (mrr). The corrections were ordered on the basis of their log likelihood ratios, from largest to smallest value, and the average reciprocal position (i.e., $1/rank$) of the first correct suggestion was calculated. They obtained a mrr value of 0.66, which indicates that an appropriate correction was likely to be found as the first or second suggestion.

Dahlmeier and Ng [2011b] analyzed the sources of wrong collocation/idiom errors in the *NUCLE* corpus and found that those which can be attributed to L1-transfer are, by far, the most common type. They developed a system for correcting collocation errors that is similar to that of Chang et al. [2008], but instead of relying on bilingual dictionaries, they automatically extracted paraphrases from a parallel Chinese-English corpus to serve as collocation candidates. The paraphrase probability is computed for each candidate given the writer's collocation and for the writer's collocation given each candidate. They adapted an approach used in phrase-based statistical translation to use these probabilities to score and rank the candidates. Their paraphrase system was compared to a baseline system that only used features based on edit distance (e.g., received critics → received criticism), homophones (e.g., this can aide → this can aid), and WordNet synonyms. The paraphrase system was substantially better than the baseline system, and when it was combined with the baseline system, there was further improvement in performance as measured by precision and mrr.

One notable way in which Chang et al. [2008] and Dahlmeier and Ng [2011b] differ from the other projects described here is that they were specifically designed to find the collocation errors of a single L1 group based on first language interference. To extend this approach, a similar use of bilingual dictionaries and/or parallel corpora would be needed for every L1.

In Chapter 7, we look at several other types of learner errors and at systems developed for languages other than English, including some non-statistical approaches to error detection.

CHAPTER 7

Different Errors and Different Approaches

Thus far, we have focused on three aspects of usage that are among the most difficult for learners to master: constructions involving articles, prepositions, and collocations. While those three dominate current NLP work in grammatical error detection, there are interesting approaches for other kinds of learner errors as well. In this chapter, we look at the uses of heuristic rules, statistical methods for detecting verb-form errors, techniques to correct spelling errors, and systems that find and repair mistakes in punctuation. After describing these systems, which target specific error types, we then turn to approaches that do not target specific errors but instead assess grammaticality over the sentence as a whole.

7.1 HEURISTIC RULE-BASED APPROACHES

As we have seen throughout this volume, statistical approaches are frequently used to develop grammatical error detection systems. The primary advantage of using these systems over rule-based approaches is that they reduce the amount of effort required to construct dozens or even hundreds of specific rules. In the case of preposition and article errors, machine learning approaches are especially advantageous because of the complexity of these errors and their interactions, as described in Chapter 3. However, for other error types, especially those where the relevant context is very local, such as determiner-noun number agreement and typographical errors, manually constructed rules can be easier to develop and may be more accurate than statistical models.

In Gamon et al. [2009], the authors note the need for different approaches for different types of errors in *ESL Assistant*:

> Preposition and article errors are at one extreme of the spectrum: large amounts of contextual information are necessary in order to arrive at a correction. On the other extreme, overregularized verb inflection is detectable without any contextual information: the form *writed* is simply one of a very limited set of forms that result in overregularization of one of the 100+ irregular verbs of English.

> In our system, we decided to take these very different error properties into account by choosing different techniques for different error types. The contextual information that is needed for preposition and article correction, for example, lends itself to

a machine-learning approach that derives generalizations about preposition and article use from large amounts of training data. Overregularized inflection, on the other hand, can be targeted by a lookup rule and a list of overregularized forms of irregular verbs.

The ETS *Criterion* system also uses the strategy of applying different approaches for different errors. Articles and prepositions primarily use large-scale statistical systems, while errors that require less contextual information, such as a subset of subject-verb agreement errors or verb formation errors, are handled by heuristic rules.

In this section, we discuss some of the systems that are, at their core, a suite of manually constructed rules, including rule-based systems for languages other than English. In 7.1.1 and 7.1.2, we describe *ALEK* (Assessing LExical Knowledge) [Chodorow and Leacock, 2000; Leacock and Chodorow, 2003], which is the rule-based component of *Criterion*, and *ESL Assistant* [Gamon et al., 2009], respectively. Both are examples of systems that make use of heuristic rules to increase the coverage of various error types, in conjunction with some of their statistical components to cover other error types such as prepositions and articles (as discussed in Chapter 5.4). Although both systems target different sets of errors, their underlying methods are essentially similar. First, a list of candidate error types is created. This can be done by manually inspecting learner corpora and noting which errors are the most prevalent, or the list can be compiled automatically by comparing word or part-of-speech tag sequence statistics from learner data with those from well-formed text. Second, sets of rules are written, usually in the form of regular expressions. The third stage involves creating filters to prevent the *n*-gram rules from generating too many false positives.

7.1.1 CRITERION SYSTEM

The motivation for the approach used in *ALEK* is that many grammatical errors have salient contextual clues that can be used to detect them. Thus, identifying if an error exists amounts to searching for patterns or clues in phrases where one element (a word or words) does not mesh with its context. *ALEK* is essentially a corpus-based bigram approach. First, a training corpus of 30 million words of well-formed American newspaper text was part-of-speech tagged. Second, bigrams consisting of part-of-speech tags and function words were extracted from the corpus and tabulated. For example, the sequence *a_AT full-time_JJ job_NN* would contribute a count to each of the bigrams *AT+JJ*, *a+JJ* and *JJ+NN*. Third, mutual information and log likelihood measures were computed for each bigram to determine which bigrams were unusually rare, or unexpected, (such as *a desks* which is represented by the bigram *a+NNS*). Next, the unexpected bigrams (as determined by a threshold) were selected and filters were manually developed to minimize false positives. Although an unexpected bigram often denotes a grammatical error, in some situations it may actually be correct. One example is *a systems analyst* where the bigram *a+NNS* would be applied. Without any context *a systems* would be incorrect, however, when it is part of a compound noun such as *a systems analyst*, the bigram is acceptable. The filters check for exceptions such as these and prevent *ALEK* from generating false positives. Essentially, *ALEK* is a combination of bigram rules created in an unsupervised fashion, and manual filters.

Twenty-one bigram rules and their filters were evaluated on a corpus of 3,300 student essays. On average, 80% of the system flags were true positives (i.e., real errors), 11% were false positives due to mistakes in tagging, and 9% were false positives due to inadequacies of the filters. Some bigrams were able to achieve 100% error identification such as *there+noun* and *nominative pronoun+to*, while others, such as *determiner+verb*, had false positive rates as high as 20%.

7.1.2 ESL ASSISTANT

ESL Assistant also contains modules consisting of heuristic rules to cover errors that its machine learning modules do not address. It targets 16 other error types with four different classes of heuristic rule-based modules: 1) verb-related modules, 2) adjective-related modules, 3) noun-related modules, and 4) preposition-related modules. Examples of verb usage covered by the system include improper use of modals (*they can *built/build a new house*), confusion between a noun and a morphologically related verb (*I will *success/succeed*), and overregularized verb inflection (**drived/drove*). Examples of adjective errors include adjective word ordering (*blue large bag* versus *large blue bag*), adjective/noun confusions (**China/Chinese people*), and predicate adjective formation (*I am *interesting/interested in many things*). The noun-related modules include methods to check for noun number (*save a lot of *labors/labor*; *not all *advertisement/advertisements*), as well methods to check for noun-of-noun errors (**door of bus* versus *bus door*). Finally, the preposition-related module checks for phrasal verb constructions (*rely *to/on a friend*) based on a fixed list of common phrasal verbs. These rules are designed to fill potential gaps in the coverage of the machine-learned module and to do so with high precision.

The heuristic rules were created by manually inspecting learner data. They are simple rules that are triggered by either lexical lookup or local part-of-speech tag sequences with a short look-ahead or look-behind to either constrain or license contexts. For example, the modal verb rule checks tensed verbs for the presence of a modal verb one or two tokens to the left, and it proposes substituting an untensed verb, e.g., changing *could danced* to *could dance*. The rule allows one adverb to the immediate left of the verb, but other part-of-speech tags cause the rule to fail. The output of these rules is filtered by a language model to reject possible false positives. The system was evaluated on three learner corpora: 10,000 sentences randomly selected from the *CLEC* corpus, 1,000 sentences randomly selected from a collection of blogs, and 1,755 sentences from Microsoft internal email. Gamon et al. [2009] reported that performance for the heuristic modules varied greatly depending on the corpus. The verb-related modules' precision ranged from 46% on web data to 53% on email data to 75% on *CLEC*.

7.1.3 OTHER HEURISTIC RULE-BASED APPROACHES

ALEK and *ESL Assistant* are just two examples of systems that make effective use of heuristic rules. Many other researchers have opted to use a rule-based approach rather than a statistical approach in the design of grammatical error detection systems. Some of these systems address verb tense errors [Omar et al., 2008], Basque determiner errors [Uria et al., 2009], Korean particle errors [Lee et al., 2009a], and Swedish collocation errors [Östling and Knutsson, 2009]. Outlining all rule-based systems goes beyond the scope of this volume; however, we will note a few key examples here.

As mentioned in Chapter 2, Bender et al. [2004] used a two-phase process to diagnosis grammatical errors and provide feedback to the writer in the form of a corrected sentence. First, mal-rules are used to map a sentence (with errors) into a correct semantic representation. Then the second phase of "aligned generation" generates a corrected version of the original sentence.

Most of the current statistical work on article and preposition errors is covered in Chapter 5, but some rule-based methods have been developed for Basque, English, and Swedish errors. This research has used linguistic analysis components such as part-of-speech taggers or broad-coverage syntactic parsers for detection and correction.

There has been considerable research into grammar checkers and into grammatical error detection for learners of Swedish over the past decade and a half. Some of the earlier work revolved around the *Grammatifix* system [Arppe, 2000; Birn, 2000], which consisted of manual rules tuned for high precision. This system, developed by Lingsoft, was used as the Swedish grammar checker in Microsoft Word 2000. Domeji et al. [2000] created a large set of hand-crafted rules that were used to produce the *Granska* error checker. Eeg-Olofsson and Knuttson [2003] developed a rule-based system to detect preposition errors for learners of Swedish that was based on part-of-speech tags assigned by a statistical trigram tagger and that used 31 rules that were written for very specific preposition errors.

One common error in German is NP agreement. Fliedner [2002] created a system based on shallow syntactic parsing to detect NP agreement errors in German with precision and recall scores at 67%. Because of the large number of inflectional rules in German and the sparseness of training data, the author used manually created grammar rules and parse ranking constraints instead of a statistical approach. The system outperformed *Grammatik*, a leading commercial general-purpose German grammar checker.

Gill and Lehal [2008] created the first automatic error detection system for Punjabi. The rule-based method performed with precision and recall of 76.8% and 87.1%, respectively, on errors such as modifier-noun agreement and subject-verb agreement. Their work also illustrates the quality of pre-processing tools for under-represented languages. Development of part-of-speech taggers and parsers for Punjabi is still in its infancy, and the results from their evaluation reflect this: in the Gill and Lehal [2008] work, the part-of-speech tagger had an accuracy of roughly 80%, whereas part-of-speech-taggers for more heavily researched languages are usually over 90%.

Uria et al. [2009] crafted a determiner correction system for Basque, which has a more complex determiner system than English and hence more determiner error types. The system is based on Constraint Grammar [Karlsson et al., 1995] and incorporates 85 rules to detect five different determiner error types. De Ilarraza et al. [2008] described a constraint grammar-based detector for postposition errors in Basque. Their system contains 30 rules targeting the five most frequent postpositions. They argue that the Basque postposition system poses some unique challenges that make it less suited to the application of data-driven methods. For example, Basque postpositions show agreement in case and number and are often distributed across two words.

7.2   MORE COMPLEX VERB FORM ERRORS

While some verb form errors (e.g., *would *went* vs. *would go*) can be very accurately corrected by heuristic rules, others are more complex and require a different solution. Like previous error types, verb form error detection and correction is dependent on the words in the verb's context and their relation to the main verb. Therefore, identifying verb form errors correctly is very important, though difficult given other errors that may arise in the context. Also, while preposition and article errors are largely influenced by factors in the local context, verb usage such as tense can be influenced by factors outside the sentence in question. For example, in the following sentences adapted from Tajiri et al. [2012]: *I had a good time this summer vacation. First I go to Kaiyukan with my friends.*, the verb *go* in the second sentence should be corrected to *went* based on the tense of the preceding sentence.

The work of Lee and Seneff [2008] focused on three cases of verb form misuse: subject-verb agreement (*He *have been living here since June*), auxiliary agreement (*He has been *live here since June*), and complementation (*He wants *live there*). In their approach, Lee and Seneff [2008] showed that verb form errors tend to perturb parse trees in a consistent manner and that by detecting these perturbations, one can better detect verb form errors. For training, they introduced verb form errors into well-formed text and then created a database of irregular parse mappings to well-formed text. For evaluation on real learner texts, they used the database to detect errors and then the Google n-gram corpus was used to filter out improbable detections. The method produced subject-verb agreement error correction of 98.9%, statistically significant over a majority baseline of 97.0%. For the other two classes (auxiliary agreement and complementation) combined, accuracy was 98.9% compared to a baseline of 98.5%, again statistically significant. Liu et al. [2010] used semantic role labeling (SRL) as the basis for their correction model. When a verb is encountered, a list of potential replacement verbs is generated for the context. Then, for each candidate, SRL features are generated and augmented with local context features (n-grams, chunking, part-of-speech tags) to be used in a perceptron classifier. They show that their method outperforms a SMT baseline derived from the work of Brockett et al. [2006]. Additionally, they showed that only using the SRL features for verb correction outperformed the standard features derived from the local context, especially in cases where verb choice was influenced by words outside the local context.

To date, the only work to tackle the problem of correcting tense and aspect errors with respect to the global context is Tajiri et al. [2012]. Similar to Gamon [2011], they framed the task as a sequence labeling one, using Conditional Random Fields (CRF). First, the model uses local features from the immediate context around the target verb. These consist of dependency features, the type of clause the target is in, the words to the left and right of the target, the tense/aspect written by the learner, and other features. Global features consist of pairs of local features, one from the target verb and another from a previous verb. The approach was trained on community-corrected data from *lang*-8. Tajiri et al. [2012] found that a CRF model outperformed maximum entropy and Support Vector Machine (SVM) models. However, performance for the CRF model was still low relative to performances on other error types in the literature. This may be a function of the difficulty of the task of tense and aspect error correction.

Research into verb correction has taken a step forward with its inclusion in two recent shared tasks: the HOO 2011 Shared Task [Dale and Kilgarriff, 2011b] and the CoNLL 2013 Shared Task on Grammatical Error Correction [Ng et al., 2013]. Both of these shared tasks are discussed in more detail in 9.1. HOO 2011 had 108 verb errors in the test set and the top performing team in terms of verb error detection [Zesch, 2011] used contextual spelling techniques, which will be discussed in more detail in the following section. The CoNLL Shared Task included verb form errors and subject-verb agreement errors. There were 246 verb errors in the test set which comprised over 7% of the total errors. Many of the same techniques discussed in Chapter 5 were used by a majority of the teams to detect the different verb errors. The top performing team [Rozovskaya et al., 2013] used a Naïve Bayes classification method similar to their methodology for article and preposition correction. They observed that one of the biggest challenges to verb correction was actually the detection phase due to pre-processing errors such as incorrect part-of-speech tags. They developed three methods for candidate selection: one that used a shallow parser to extract candidate verbs, one that expanded the list given a set of predefined part-of-speech tags, and a third which derived a list of verbs and their lemmas from the Gigaword corpus. The third method was used in the final system and produced an F-score of 24.51 on the test set. Xing et al. [2013] had the second best performance at 22.39 F-score and used a set of heuristic rules to detect verb form errors and a classification-based approach for subject-verb agreement which relied on lexical and part-of-speech tag features from the local context.

7.3   SPELLING ERRORS

Spelling errors fall into two categories, that of non-words and that of confusing homophones or near-homophones (such as *affect, effect* and *too, two*)—also called real-word spelling errors. Spelling errors of both types abound in both native and non-native writing. There has been a wealth of NLP work in the area of spelling correction for decades (cf. Kukich [1992], Hirst and Budanitsky [2005], and Heift and Schulze [2007] for comprehensive overviews).

In the case of confused words, the result is often a grammatical error. Briefly, spell checking for homophones and near-homophones can be categorized into three classes:

- **Semantic Approaches**: The work by Hirst and Budanitsky [2005] was based on the assumption that real-word spelling errors (such as *hole* for *hope* in "It is my sincere *hole* that you will recover quickly.") are less likely to be semantically related to the text than the writer's intended word is. Their method works by generating real-word candidate spelling corrections for the target word and then, for each candidate, calculating its semantic distance from the context. If a candidate correction is semantically closer, then the original word is marked as an error.

- **Disambiguation Approaches**: Several methods [Carlson et al., 2001; Golding, 1995; Golding and Roth, 1996] have taken a different approach by treating the task of detecting homophone errors as a disambiguation task. In this case, the target words and their common confusions (such as *affect, effect*) must be predefined. A statistical classifier is then used to select the best one given the context.

- **Probabilistic Approaches**: Islam and Inkpen [2009] used the trigrams from the Google n-gram corpus to improve recall in homophone error detection. Whitelaw et al. [2009] used n-grams from the web to create an unsupervised spelling corrector. Their approach is novel in that it makes use of spelling mistakes commonly found on the web, so their model takes into account both negative and positive spelling examples.

While there are many systems devoted to non-word spelling correction, what unites the vast majority of them is that they are directed toward native speakers; spelling correction tools designed for language learners are currently rare. However, interest in this area is growing. In an early study, Rimrott and Heift [2005] evaluated the Microsoft *Word 2003* spelling corrector on German learner texts and found that only 52% of the errors were corrected; this is substantially lower than performance on texts written by German native speakers.

In further analysis, Rimrott and Heift [2008] classified learner competence errors into three categories: lexical, morphological, and phonological. Lexical errors are the result of the writer not knowing the appropriate translation of the target word. Morphological errors involve incorrectly inflected or derived words—including what we have elsewhere called overregularized inflection such as writing *goed* instead of *went*. Phonological errors are confusions caused by either the native or the target language. Rimrott and Heift [2008] further classify these competence errors by edit distance—the number of keystrokes it takes to correct the misspelling. Their classification is (1) edit distance equals one or (2) is greater than one. Again, they found that fewer learner errors are corrected than native errors. While the generic spell checkers did quite well on errors with an edit distance of one, accuracy dropped when the edit distance is greater than one.

Flor and Futagi [2012] reported that the ConSpel spell checker, while not specifically designed for language learners, has almost the same rate of success for native and non-native English speakers. This does not necessarily contradict previous studies because ConSpel makes a special effort to correct misspellings with an edit distance of greater than one.

A great aid to the growing research in non-native spelling errors is the creation of learner spelling error corpora [Bestgen and Granger, 2011; Flor and Futagi, 2013]. Mitton and Okada [2007] based a spell corrector for Japanese learners of English on an analysis of learner spelling errors. Sakaguchi et al. [2012b] used the annotated spelling errors in *CLC* to train a spell correction algorithm that is done in tandem with part-of-speech tagging.

7.4   PUNCTUATION ERRORS

Mastering the use of commas, hyphens, and periods can be challenging for both native and non-native speakers. Punctuation error detection is also an area of research that has been investigated only sparingly. Dahlmeier and Ng [2012a] developed a set of rules for correcting punctuation as part of their beam-search decoder system for error correction. Other researchers have trained statistical classifiers to correct comma and hyphen errors.

Israel et al. [2012] developed an annotation scheme, annotated a corpus, and developed a system for detecting comma usage errors made in learner writing. They first compiled a set of 15 rules of comma usage found in a number of style manuals and used them as the basis for their annotation scheme. Results of the annotation showed that about 15% of the commas found in the essays of native speakers and in the essays of non-native speakers were judged to be used incorrectly. For both groups of writers, an even greater problem than cases of misuse was the failure to use commas where they were needed. To detect both types of comma errors, extraneous and missing, Israel et al. [2012] developed a CRF classifier that was trained on well-formed text. In addition to local features, the classifier used "distance features" that encode how far the current word is from the beginning and end of the sentence, and how far it is from the previous and following coordinating conjunctions. The results for comma error correction in non-native writing showed 0.94 precision with 0.32 recall, and for native writing, 0.85 precision with 0.20 recall.

Cahill et al. [2013a] noted that while hyphen errors are rather infrequent and are often less serious than other types of errors, they can nevertheless affect the quality of writing. To detect and correct errors of hyphen omission, the researchers used a maximum entropy classifier and features from the local context around the position between two words. In addition, a feature indicated if the two words appeared hyphenated in the Collins dictionary, and another feature represented the proportion of the occurrences of the word pair that were hyphenated in Wikipedia. The classifier was trained on newspaper text, on hyphen error text that was automatically extracted from revisions of Wikipedia, and on both. Results for precision in learner essays showed better performance for the classifiers than for baselines that used only the presence of the hyphenated word pair in the dictionary or in Wikipedia.

7.5   DETECTION OF UNGRAMMATICAL SENTENCES

While prior work has focused on finding specific errors and giving learners feedback about them, the learner might also benefit from simply being told that a sentence is ill-formed. A system that can detect ungrammatical sentences could be used in other applications as well, for example, to improve the quality of data mined from the web or other noisy corpora by identifying and removing ill-formed sentences.

Table 7.1: Examples of Grammatical/Ungrammatical Sentence Pairs

Early work on identifying ungrammatical sentences was rule-based (such as Heidorn [2000] and Bender et al. [2004]). By contrast, Sun et al. [2007] took an approach that is not rule-based but which also differs from the statistical methods described in Chapters 5 and 6. Instead of developing features that describe the context surrounding a specific error, they extracted frequently occurring sequences (*labeled sequential patterns* or LSPs) from a corpus of well-formed text and a corpus of ungrammatical, learner texts. LSPs consist of a sequence of contiguous or non-contiguous tokens and/or part-of-speech tags. By using a sequence mining algorithm, they were able to generate a large database of common patterns that occur in both corpora. The intuition is that if an LSP predominantly occurs in a corpus of well-formed texts, it is probably a *correct* construction. Conversely, if an LSP predominantly occurs in a corpus of learner texts, it is probably an example of an *error* construction. Each LSP has associated with it confidence and support values which describe how well-attested the LSP is. These values make it easy to prune LSPs that appear in both corpora regularly. With this approach, one can automatically identify common learner errors such as a singular determiner followed by a plural noun and a past tense verb preceded by the infinitive marker *to*, and distinguish them from common well-formed sequences such as *would* followed by an untensed verb. After some filtering, each sequential pattern is converted into a binary feature and is the input to a machine learning classifier in conjunction with other features, such as language model perplexity, syntactic score, and function word density. The method was tested on a corpus of Japanese learner text, yielding an accuracy of 81.8%, and on a corpus of Chinese learner text, with an accuracy of 79.8%. It was also shown to identify ill-formed sentences better than Microsoft *Word* and *ALEK* when both of those systems were recalibrated for the task by marking the sentence as ungrammatical whenever the respective system found one or more errors in the sentence.

Lee et al. [2007] developed a statistical method for grammaticality detection to investigate whether data derived from machine translation could be used as an effective substitute for learner data. An SVM classifier was trained to flag a sentence as either grammatical or ungrammatical based on five features—language model perplexity, parse score, parse tree derivation frequency, head-noun determiner errors, and a simple collocation error model. Their method performed at 66.4% accuracy on a corpus of Japanese texts when trained on a combination of well-formed and learner texts. When the learner texts were replaced by texts generated by a machine translation system, performance dropped to 59.0%. The same system was also applied to a related task of ranking sentences with the same meaning, based on how native sounding they are. The system trained on machine translation data actually performed better than one trained on learner data (76.2% to 74.6%, respectively). This shows that, in some domains, a large training corpus of learner writing is not necessarily required for high performance.

Alam et al. [2006] also tackled the task of identifying sentences with at least one error, in both English and Bangla. The method used a language model (based on 5,000 words from a Bangladeshi newspaper) consisting of trigram part-of-speech-tag sequences over the target sentence. If the probability of the sentence did not meet a threshold, the sentence was flagged as an error. They evaluated the method on English and Bangla, achieving 63% and 53% accuracy, respectively, when using sentences that had been part-of-speech tagged manually. They tested the grammar checker with an automatic Bangla part-of-speech tagger on a small set of 34 sentences and found performance dropped to 38%.

Finally, Gamon [2011] used high order sequence models to detect the presence of any type of error in a sentence. As we have seen in the previous two chapters, most work in error detection and correction has focused on models for correcting specific errors. The advantage of Gamon's approach, and machine translation based approaches to be discussed in Chapter 9, is that they can detect any error type with a single model. The idea is to treat error detection as a sequence modeling task (such as that commonly used in part-of-speech tagging and Named Entity Recognition), which employs dozens of language model features, string features, and linguistic analysis features. Several of the language model features in Gamon [2011] were novel in that they encoded different methods of measuring changes in "grammatical goodness" from token to token. The intuition behind the method is that ungrammatical sequences in a sentence should have relatively lower language model scores than grammatical sequences. Note that this differs from other approaches considered here as it goes beyond a holistic evaluation of the sentence and is capable of identifying one or more spans that may correspond to the locations of errors.

7.6 SUMMARY

In the previous two chapters, we reviewed approaches designed to detect article, preposition, and collocation errors, some of the most frequent mistakes made by learners of English. In this chapter, we described systems for finding and correcting other common learner errors ranging from incorrect verb forms to spelling and punctuation mistakes. Heuristic rule-based methods (as in *ALEK* and some modules of *ESL Assistant*) have proven to work quite well for many of these error types. The last few years have also witnessed a modest increase in the development of error detection systems for learners of languages other than English. However, for many languages, progress has often been hampered by a lack of available resources in the target language, such as corpora and NLP pre-processing tools. Finally, we described statistical classifiers designed to distinguish between grammatical and ungrammatical sentences as a whole without targeting specific kinds of errors. We hope that this chapter has provided a useful look at the many lines of research worth exploring beyond English article, preposition, and collocation errors.

CHAPTER 8

Annotating Learner Errors

The cornerstone of any NLP evaluation is the manual annotation of data to create a gold standard evaluation set. With this set, one can quickly compare a system's predictions to the annotators' judgments and report performance. Annotation tasks can range from simply labeling a picture or website, to assigning part-of-speech tags, or to more complicated tasks such as discourse structure labeling. Simple tasks may require just one annotator, but more complex tasks often require two or more annotators since judgments are more likely to differ. While there has been considerable emphasis in the field placed on system development, there has actually been little attention paid to developing best practices for annotation. In this chapter, we cover the issues surrounding error annotation, describe two different annotation schemes in detail, and describe work on ameliorating some of the problems that researchers have previously encountered when annotating learner productions for errors.

8.1 ISSUES WITH LEARNER ERROR ANNOTATION

Here we consider some issues related to the cost and reliability of annotation, in particular, questions concerning how many annotators to use, how many error types to annotate, and whether annotation should be exhaustive or based on samples of an error detection system's output. We also present a brief survey of some software tools designed to facilitate the annotation process.

8.1.1 NUMBER OF ANNOTATORS

When using just one trained annotator, that annotator's judgments become the gold standard for system evaluation. Time and cost are the two most important reasons why so much research has relied on judgments of a single annotator, because multiple annotations of the same learner text multiplies the resources that are required. This is especially the case for annotating learner text because targeted error types can be sparse, even in beginner and intermediate learner writing. For example, errors of preposition usage in learner English occur at rates as low as 1 in 10 prepositions in the text. Thus, in order to collect a corpus of 1,000 preposition errors, each annotator needs to make judgments on more than 10,000 prepositions. Tetreault and Chodorow [2008b] reported that it would take about 80 hours for one of their trained annotators to identify and correct 1,000 preposition errors.

Tetreault and Chodorow [2008b] showed that relying solely on a single annotator leads to unstable precision and recall measures of system performance because of low inter-annotator reliability. Lee et al. [2009b] found similar variability of kappa in a related experiment on articles.

For some errors where rules are clearly defined, such as subject-verb agreement or subject-verb-object word order, it may be acceptable to use a single annotator. However, usage errors such as prepositions and collocations, where there are no overarching rules, can be harder to annotate and thus may require multiple annotators to collect a range of judgments. Tables 8.1 and 8.2 show examples for collocations and prepositions, respectively, where two trained annotators disagreed on whether to flag the construction as an error.

Table 8.1: Examples of Verb-Noun Collocations where Two Annotators Disagreed

Table 8.2: Examples of Preposition Usage where Two Annotators Disagreed

The upshot is that for error types that are not driven by clear-cut rules and where native speakers do not always agree, using multiple annotators and having them come to a consensus in the cases where they disagree may create a less biased annotation scheme. Unfortunately, using multiple annotators to annotate the same contexts requires more resources than using just one. In Section 8.3, we discuss some methods of reducing annotation costs when using multiple annotators.

8.1.2   ANNOTATION SCHEMES

Lüdeling et al. [2005] argue that an annotation scheme for learner corpora should ideally be able to encode multiple corrections for each error, do so on multiple levels, such as syntactic, morphological, and orthographic, and accommodate errors involving sequences of tokens as well as single-token errors. The authors describe three general types of annotation structures typically found in learner corpora and evaluate them with respect to these desired properties. Tabular schemes annotate tokens. Although they can accommodate multiple levels by using multiple tags (e.g., *goed/morph/went* to mark a token with its error type and correction), they are not appropriate for annotating sequences. Tree-based annotation is commonly represented using XML or similar mark-up. It can handle sequences of tokens, but it cannot handle overlapping ranges of tokens, for example in alternative corrections of an error. Multilayer standoff annotation is not inserted into the text but instead is coded separately. It provides the greatest flexibility and satisfies

Lüdeling et al.'s criteria. The HOO 2011 and 2012 shared tasks both used standoff annotation in their training data [Dale et al., 2012].

Another issue pertains to the scope of the error annotation. Much work in error detection uses detailed annotation schemes which aim to identify as many as 50 different kinds of errors or more. The advantage of this is that a wide range of errors can be marked at one time. One problem, however, is that an annotator has to remember many types of error tags and the rules for using them, which can slow the annotation process and lower inter-annotator agreement. More recently, some annotation schemes have focused on a single error type. Even focusing on just one error type, there are still questions to be answered, in particular, how to define the error type of interest and decide what falls into this category and what does not.

8.1.3   HOW TO CORRECT AN ERROR

The best way to annotate an error depends on the goal of the project. If the goal is to target specific error types with the intention of evaluating error detection systems, then the best method may be to identify each error and supply a correction for it. As we have seen, though, there are often many ways to correct an error. For example, a singular count noun without a determiner, such as *book*, may be rewritten with an indefinite article (*a book*), a definite article (*the book*), or as a plural (*books*). Annotation becomes even more complicated when there are other errors in the context of the target. In those cases, it may be more practical to ask the annotator to make a best guess or to flag the context as difficult to judge, or to indicate the confidence in their judgment. Another way, though more laborious, is to list the different ways the context can be repaired and/or provide a fluent rewrite of the context.

In some instances, the local context is insufficient to decide if an error has occurred and, if it has, which correction is best. This is especially true of errors involving articles, where document-level features are important for representing the prior context. Specifically, when first mentioned in a document, a noun is more likely to be modified by "a," and on subsequent occurrences it is more likely to be modified by "the." For this reason, Han et al. [2004] used features to represent prior occurrences of a noun in the document. Lee et al. [2009b] looked at factors that affect human annotator agreement when correcting English article and noun number errors, such as "He liked book," which could be corrected by replacing "book" with "a book," "the book," "books," or "the books." They found improved agreement and kappa when annotators were able to view the two sentences that preceded the sentence containing the error.

8.1.4   ANNOTATION APPROACHES

When designing an annotation task, one must decide which annotation *approach* to employ. This decision is not independent of how one plans to evaluate the system. The choice is often related to two factors: (1) Is the error such that a range of judgments is needed? (2) What are the time and cost constraints? Table 8.3 summarizes the advantages and disadvantages of three approaches for evaluating error detection systems. The exhaustive approach refers to the method of annotating all of the errors, or all instances of an error type, in an evaluation corpus. Its advantage is that the annotated corpus can be reused to evaluate the same system or compare multiple systems. However, if the corpus is very large and multiple annotators are required, it can be very costly and time-consuming. To ease this burden, Andersen [2011] developed a semi-automated system for annotating the *CLC*. It automatically detects frequently recurring errors involving spelling, morphology, and contextually inappropriate words (*I *thing that*), and it automatically corrects a great many of these. This increases considerably the overall speed of annotation. The human annotator can quickly verify the automatic tags and corrections, making more time available to focus on errors that cannot be detected or corrected automatically. The verification approach (as used in Gamon et al. [2008]) refers to the method of simply checking the acceptability of a system's error flags or corrections compared to what the learner wrote. Verification is more efficient than the exhaustive approach because fewer judgments are required. But the disadvantage of verification is that it does not permit estimation of recall. Finally, the sampling approach (which will be discussed in detail in Section 8.3.1) can be used to *estimate* both precision and recall using a fraction of the resources of the exhaustive approach. Both verification and sampling approaches have the disadvantage of requiring re-verification or re-annotation for system retesting and comparison. However, both methods make it possible to assess system performance on a new corpus relatively quickly.

Table 8.3: Comparison of Annotation Approaches

8.1.5   ANNOTATION TOOLS

While there are no agreed upon annotation standards, there are also no standard annotation tools for error detection and correction. The preposition annotation work in Tetreault and Chodorow [2008b] was done by simply using a Microsoft *Excel* spreadsheet instead of special-purpose annotation software. However, annotation tools can expedite the annotation process by allowing annotators to click buttons for a particular error code and have the tool generate the annotations automatically. One general purpose annotation tool that allows a user to separate different annotation schemes related to the same text into levels is the MMAX2 tool.[1] For their work on preposition and article error detection, Rozovskaya and Roth [2010a] developed a different Java-based annotation tool where users could select the best error tag and correction from a check-button-enabled list that included tags for noun number, verb form, word form, spelling, and other error types. Aldabe et al. [2007] created the "Error Editor Tool" to assist their research on error detection for Basque writers. Dahlmeier et al. [2013] developed their own internet-based tool, WAMP, for their annotation of *NUCLE*. Andersen [2011] produced a tool that is especially well-suited to semi-automatic annotation. It shows the annotator the automatically generated error tags and corrections, which can be reviewed and changed if necessary.

8.2   ANNOTATION SCHEMES

In this section, we review some examples of annotation schemes. Granger [2003] is an example of a scheme that aims to identify many errors at the same time. By contrast, Tetreault and Chodorow [2008b] is an example of an approach that annotates a single error type to the exclusion of all others.

8.2.1   EXAMPLES OF COMPREHENSIVE ANNOTATION SCHEMES

The value of a learner corpus for linguistic research and for NLP system development depends largely on its size and the quality of its error annotation. Granger [2003] has argued that an error annotation scheme should be, among other things, consistent and informative. Consistency here means reliable or used in a consistent manner, and, as we have seen, this can be a serious problem, especially for annotating usage errors involving articles, prepositions, and collocations. One approach is to provide the annotator with extensive guidance in the form of a manual that specifies, in detail, the criteria for using each error tag. Despite such resources, annotators often have to make arbitrary decisions about which tag to use, although most schemes do permit annotators to tag an error using multiple codes. Most annotation schemes also require the annotator to supply a correction for the error, but this too is dependent on the annotator's choice of tag. Nicholls [2003] describes the philosophy used in tagging the *CLC* when faced with ambiguous cases as trying "to keep as close as possible to the student's original text." This requires the error codes to be viewed as forming a kind of hierarchy. For example, a sentence that begins *He said me that ...*

---

[1]http://www.eml-research.de/english/research/nlp/download/mmax.php

could be tagged for a missing preposition (*He said to me that ...*) or for an incorrect verb (*He told me that ...*), but the former correction keeps the text closer to the original.

The informativeness of annotations depends on their granularity, or how much information they encode. The set of error tags generally reflects a taxonomy, as in the system used for *ICLE* [Dagneaux et al., 1996; Granger et al., 2002b], which has major categories of form, punctuation, grammar, lexico-grammar, register, word (extraneous, omitted, or wrong word order), and style. These categories are combined with part of speech and more specific error types, such as tense and countable/uncountable, to yield tags like GVT for a Grammar-Verb-Tense error and XNPR for leXico-grammar-Noun-PReposition error. The need to be informative can lead to many tag types, which must be balanced against the need of the annotator for a tag set that does not impose too heavy a cognitive load. These tags were not designed for use by statistical classifiers, so they may require some additional processing. For example, in the annotation scheme for *ICLE*, there are potentially seven error tags that can apply to prepositions depending on the types of phrases in which they appear and the types of objects that they have.

Diaz-Negrillo and Fernández-Dominguez [2006] provide a survey of twelve error tagging systems and focus on four of the best known and best documented ones. They note that across these systems, the number of error tags ranges from about 30 to as many as 100. With a large number of tags for the annotator to keep in mind and with many decisions to be made in selecting each tag, the need for informativeness is likely to conflict with the need for consistency. Recently, Dahlmeier et al. [2013] used 27 tag categories to annotate errors in the *NUCLE* corpus. They reported average kappas between their annotators of 0.39 for identifying the presence of an error, 0.55 for assigning the same category to an error, and 0.48 for assigning the same category and the same correction to an error. The researchers noted that these values are relatively low and that there was also a substantial amount of variability in the kappa values depending on which pair of annotators were being compared.

8.2.2   EXAMPLE OF A TARGETED ANNOTATION SCHEME

In contrast to the schemes used in the *CLC* or in Granger's work, a focused tag set that deals with only one error type can be developed. By focusing on a single error type, the expectation is that annotators will be more focused and therefore more consistent in their judgments.

An example is the *cascading preposition annotation* scheme in Tetreault and Chodorow [2008b]. A variant of this scheme was used in Rozovskaya and Roth [2010a] as well. Annotators were shown sentences randomly selected from student essays, with every preposition in the sentence highlighted. The annotator was first asked to indicate if there were any spelling errors within the context of the preposition (± 2-word window and the governing verb, if there was one). Next, the annotator was asked to identify other problems within the context of the preposition: noting determiner or number errors, and any other grammatical errors (for example, wrong verb form). The reason for having the annotators check spelling and grammar is that other parts of a grammatical error detection system would be responsible for these error types. One could also design two types of system evaluations: one where the system is evaluated on prepositions without any errors in the context, and one where errors exist. For an example of a sentence that contains multiple spelling, grammatical, and collocation errors, consider the following: *In consion, for some reasons, museums, particuraly known travel place, get on many people.* A spelling error follows the preposition *in*, and a collocation error surrounds *on*.

The annotator then assigned the writer's preposition to one of four categories: (1) extraneous preposition error, (2) preposition choice error, (3) acceptable preposition , and (4) acceptable preposition but the context also licenses other acceptable prepositions. In the second and fourth cases, the annotator was also required to supply the alternate prepositions. Finally, the annotator indicated the confidence in their judgment on a two-point scale (high confidence and low confidence).

Tetreault and Chodorow [2008b] found that their two annotators had an average kappa of 0.63, which is considered substantial. More telling is what was found when the system's judgments were compared to those of the annotators. When comparing the system's output with one annotator and treating that annotator's judgments as the gold standard, the performance of the system was 78% precision and 26% recall. However, when comparing with the second annotator, performance was 68% precision and 21% recall. That means when just one annotator is used, system performance can be skewed by as much as 10% precision and 5% recall.

8.3 PROPOSALS FOR EFFICIENT ANNOTATION

When using multiple annotators for error annotation, there is the possibility of creating an adjudicated set, or at least calculating the variability of system evaluation. However, annotation with multiple annotators has its own disadvantages in terms of time and cost. Even using one annotator to produce a sizable evaluation corpus of preposition errors can require considerable resources. In this section, we discuss three methods that help circumvent the problems associated with multiple annotators and large-scale annotation: sampling, crowdsourcing, and mining online revision logs.

8.3.1 SAMPLING APPROACH WITH MULTIPLE ANNOTATORS

The work of Tetreault and Chodorow [2008b] describes a sampling approach that makes it possible to efficiently evaluate a system so that multiple annotators can be used and, especially important for errors with low error rates, so that more possible errors can be annotated. The procedure is inspired by the one described in Chodorow and Leacock [2000] and has commonalities with Active Learning approaches [Dagan and Engelson, 1995; Engelson and Dagan, 1996]. The central idea is to skew the annotation corpus so that it contains a greater proportion of errors. The result is that an annotator checks more potential errors and spends less time evaluating cases where target constructions are used correctly.

There are two requirements for the sampling approach: a system for detecting the error in question and a large learner corpus. First, the system is run over the learner corpus and flags each target construction as being correct or incorrect. Two sub-corpora are then created: one consisting of the target constructions marked by the system as correct (*OK*), and another consisting of the target constructions marked by the system as incorrect (*error*). A typical verification approach would have the annotator review only the *error* sub-corpus. However, this does not make it possible to estimate recall since it is not known how many errors are missed by the system in the *OK* sub-corpus. To address this, random samples are drawn from each sub-corpus and are combined into an annotation set that is given to a "blind" annotator who does not know the system's judgments. A higher sampling rate should be used for the *error* sub-corpus to enrich the annotation set with a larger proportion of errors than is found in the test corpus as a whole. In their experiments, Tetreault and Chodorow [2008b] randomly selected 75% of the target constructions from the *error* sub-corpus and 16% from the *OK* corpus. With the new annotation set, the annotator(s) annotated the data, and their judgments were compared to the system's. Precision and recall were estimated using the TPs, FPs, and FNs from the comparison with the annotation, and then those counts were weighted by the sample proportions and the relative sizes of the sub-corpora.

As a proof of concept for the approach, Tetreault and Chodorow [2008b] compared the precision and recall estimates obtained by using the sampling approach to precision and recall figures from using the exhaustive approach. For this task, a large corpus of TOEFL essays was split into two sets: first, a set of 8,269 preposition contexts (exhaustive approach corpus) to be annotated using the scheme described in 8.2.2, and second, a set of 22,000 preposition contexts to be analyzed using the sampling approach (sampling corpus). Using the exhaustive approach, the sampling corpus of 22,000 prepositions would normally take several weeks for two annotators to double annotate and then adjudicate. After this corpus was divided into *OK* and *error* sub-corpora, the two sub-corpora were proportionally sampled, resulting in an annotation set of 750 preposition contexts (500 contexts from the *OK* sub-corpus and 250 contexts from the *error* sub-corpus). The 750 contexts required roughly 6 hours for annotation, which is substantially less than the exhaustive approach.

Using the exhaustive annotation approach, precision and recall were 80% and 12%, respectively. Using the sampling approach, precision and recall estimates were 79% and 14%, respectively, thus suggesting that the sampling approach can be used as an alternative to exhaustive annotation. In short, the sampling approach is intended to alleviate the burden on annotators when faced with the task of having to rate several thousand errors of a particular type to produce a sizable error corpus.

8.3.2 CROWDSOURCING ANNOTATIONS

Crowdsourcing is the process of collecting large numbers of judgments from untrained people online. Over the last five years it has become an extremely popular tool for a myriad of needs ranging from research experiments to marketing to outsourcing simple tasks. Amazon provides a crowdsourcing service called the *Mechanical Turk* (*AMT*)[2] which allows "requesters" (companies, researchers, etc.) to post simple tasks (known as Human Intelligence Tasks, or HITs) to the

---

[2]http://aws.amazon.com/mturk/

AMT website for untrained annotators to perform for payments as low as $0.01 in many cases [Sheng et al., 2008]. *AMT* has been shown to be an effective tool for annotation and evaluation in NLP tasks ranging from word similarity judgments and emotion detection [Snow et al., 2008] to machine translation [Callison-Burch, 2009]. In these cases, a handful of untrained *AMT* workers (or Turkers) were found to be as effective as trained annotators, but with the advantage of being considerably faster and less expensive. Given the success of using *AMT* in other areas of NLP, Tetreault et al. [2010a] carried out two pilot annotation studies with *AMT*: preposition selection and preposition error annotation. They found that, at a fraction of the time and cost, using *AMT* makes it possible to acquire high quality judgments from *multiple* untrained annotators without sacrificing reliability. A summary of the results of their two experiments can be seen in Table 8.4.

In a preposition selection experiment [Tetreault et al., 2010a] where one tries to predict the writer's preposition by filling in a blank, the most frequently given response from a set of Turkers was compared to the response of a trained annotator. Results showed that the majority judgment of only three Turkers was needed to match the reliability of a trained annotator. In a second experiment, to examine the reliability of Turker preposition error judgments, Turkers were presented with a preposition highlighted in a sentence from learner text, and were instructed to judge its usage as either *correct*, *incorrect*, or *too hard to judge given the words surrounding it*. The set consisted of 152 prepositions in total, with 20 judgments per preposition. A screenshot of a sample HIT for this task is shown in Figure 8.1.

Because there was no gold standard for the error detection task, kappa was used to compare Turker responses to those of three trained annotators. Between pairs of trained annotators, kappa ranged from 0.57 to 0.65, for a mean kappa of 0.61. Kappa was also calculated for the comparisons of the most frequent Turker response to that of each annotator for samples of various sizes ranging from $N = 1$ to $N = 18$ Turkers. At sample size $N = 13$, the average kappa was 0.61, identical to the mean found among the trained annotators. In short, in the first experiment three Turkers were required to match the reliability of trained annotators on the preposition selection task, and in the second experiment 13 Turkers were required for the harder task of preposition error detection. In a replication and extension of this work, Madnani et al. [2011] and Tetreault et al. [2013] used the CrowdFlower service[3] for their crowdsourced judgments. CrowdFlower uses AMT, but it provides additional quality control by screening out workers who are untrustworthy in terms of their responses to requester-supplied "gold" items, i.e., items that should be clear cases yielding a high degree of consensus. With this quality control in place, only five worker judgments, instead of 12 or 13 as in previous studies, were needed to match the kappa found between the trained annotators in the preposition error detection task. Similarly, without gold, nine judgments were needed to match the trained annotators' reliability for article error detection, but with gold, only five were required. In the task of collocation error detection, the numbers were four judgments without gold but just three judgments needed when gold items were used for quality control.

---

[3]http://crowdflower.com/

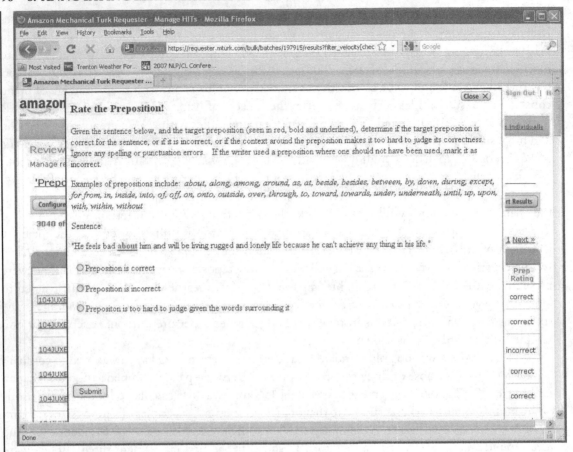

Figure 8.1: Sample HIT for error detection task .

Table 8.4: Summary of Time and Cost for Tetreault et al. [2010a] AMT Experiments

Task	Number of Preps	Judgments per Prep	Cost	Total Cost	Total Turkers	Total Time
Selection	194	10	$0.02	$48.50	49	0.5 hrs
Detection	152	20	$0.02	$76.00	74	6 hrs

These experiments not only show that crowdsourcing can be used as an effective alternative annotation source, but they also open up the possibility of fundamentally changing the way in which usage errors are annotated and represented. Because multiple judgments are easily acquired through crowdsourcing, usage errors can be viewed as values on a continuous, rather than a categorical, scale. Instead of treating the task of error detection as a "black or white" distinction, where a preposition is either correct or incorrect, usage judgments can be treated as a graded measure. For example, if 90% or more of annotators judge a preposition to be an error, the high agreement is strong evidence that this is a clear case of an error. A system should be penalized greatly for missing such an error. Conversely, agreement levels closer to 50% would indicate that the use of a particular preposition is not clear-cut, and, accordingly, an automated error detection system should not be greatly penalized for failing to flag the error. Madnani et al. [2011] show how the formulas for precision and recall (see Chapter 4 in this volume) can be modified to produce weighted precision and weighted recall that reflect the graded nature of usage judgments. They argue that weighted metrics provide fairer and more stable measures of system performance than the traditional ones. As discussed in Section 4.4.3, an additional benefit of using graded error annotations is that they can facilitate cross-system evaluation.

There are several research avenues for using crowdsourcing for annotation and evaluation. One can experiment with different guidelines and instructions to improve inter-annotator reliability and reduce the number of Turkers required for a task. Other filtering techniques include screening out Turkers who are non-native speakers of English by using a questionnaire [Callison-Burch, 2009] and weighting Turkers' responses [Snow et al., 2008]. Finally, an obvious extension of the work described above is to investigate the number of annotators necessary to annotate other kinds of errors.

8.3.3   MINING ONLINE COMMUNITY-DRIVEN REVISION LOGS

NLP researchers have begun using the information available in revision logs of collaborative online resources (Wikipedia, for example) to obtain data for such tasks as spelling correction [Max and Wisniewski, 2010; Zesch, 2012] and lexical error detection [Nelken and Yamangil, 2008]. The advantage of mining revision logs is that it provides, at no expense, a much larger amount of annotated data than can be gathered through standard annotation or crowdsourcing methods making it a possible source of *training* data for large statistical classifiers and not just *evaluation* data, which tend to be smaller. An additional advantage is that the data is dynamic: it is constantly growing and being edited. Of course, community-oriented error correction has the downside that some errors may be incorrectly annotated, making the corpus noisier than ones derived from more standard methods. However, the work of Cahill et al. [2013b] shows that statistical models trained on this noisy Wikipedia data outperform those trained on much cleaner, yet smaller amounts of well-annotated data. To address the noise issue, they compared each revision of a Wikipedia article with the immediately previous revision and then computed all the edit chains in which a single preposition was inserted, changed, or deleted (e.g., *in* → *of* → *on*). For all non-circular chains of this type, they extracted the first and last elements (e.g., in/on), which were considered to represent a preposition error and its correction, respectively. In this way, they were able to automatically extract approximately 2 million sentences annotated for preposition errors and corrections.

In addition to Wikipedia, the *lang-8* website has proven to be a valuable source of error-annotated learner data. It is a free language-exchange social networking site where those learning a language can post their writing and native speakers of that language can provide feedback in the form of corrections and comments. With well over 200,000 users, there are hundreds of thousands of corrected errors that can be mined from the revision logs. Another interesting property of the website is that it does not focus specifically on English learners; there are data for learners of several other languages (most notably Japanese). This resource has proven effective as training data for several different studies. Mizumoto et al. [2011] used a collection of over 800,000 Japanese learner sentences for automatic whole sentence correction. Tajiri et al. [2012] extracted 750,000 corrected verb phrases from English learner sentences, and with this large data resource, they created a classifier for verb tense/aspect correction. Cahill et al. [2013b] extracted 53,000 English preposition errors from the revision logs and used those data in two ways: to train a system on correct and incorrect examples of usage, and to develop a corpus of artificial errors. When tested on the *CLC-FCE* corpus [Yannakoudakis et al., 2011], the model trained on the corpus of artificial errors outperformed all other measures, including models trained on Wikipedia and well-formed data.

8.4   SUMMARY

Many of the schemes for annotating learner errors were developed primarily for language instruction and corpus linguistics research. They target dozens of error types, but they are not intended for use in training and evaluating statistical classifiers. More recently, NLP researchers have designed a number of their own targeted annotation schemes to evaluate their systems' performance on a single kind of error. One important challenge that has yet to be adequately addressed is the need for agreed-upon standards for both comprehensive and targeted annotation. Another important issue in annotation concerns the number of judgments available for each potential error. Because of the time and expense required for annotating, many evaluation corpora are only singly annotated, but studies have shown that reliability of these annotations can be quite low, especially for word usage errors. To address the time and cost issues, and thus the feasibility of having multiple annotators, several techniques have been developed, such as utilizing the verification method and the sampling approach, and more recently, using crowdsourcing and revision mining.

Crowdsourcing provides a way to obtain a large number of annotator judgments which, in turn, opens up the possibility of treating correctness of usage as a continuous variable rather than as a dichotomous one. Mining community-driven revision logs, such as those of Wikipedia, makes it possible to acquire enough annotated errors and corrections to use for robust training as well as for evaluation. Because many of these developments are quite recent, we believe that prospects are bright for further improvements in annotation for error detection/correction. Future success in this field will likely depend upon it.

CHAPTER 9

Emerging Directions

Since the first edition of this volume in 2010, there have been several exciting developments and emerging directions in the field of automated grammatical error correction. In this chapter we highlight several areas in which progress has been made and areas where the field can still improve.

In 2010, one of the biggest impediments to progress was the lack of a common corpus as well as common evaluation standards. This made it very difficult, if not at times impossible, to reliably compare different methods for error correction. To address this problem, the community has come together since 2011 on three shared tasks in grammatical error correction. Shared tasks have the advantage that all participants use the same training and test sets, and the same evaluation metrics. In Section 9.1 we discuss the organization and results of the three shared tasks. We then turn to two approaches that deserve mention in this volume. Error correction methods based on advances in machine translation have been proposed multiple times over the years, but we believe that their potential has not yet been fully realized. In addition, research has established that crowdsourcing can be turned into a near real-time source for help in the editing of texts—a new direction that has yet to be exploited explicitly for the correction of non-native errors. These two approaches are covered in Sections 9.2 and 9.3, respectively. Finally, in Section 9.4 we discuss recent research into the short- and long-term effects of automated error correction feedback on learners' writing.

9.1 SHARED TASKS IN GRAMMATICAL ERROR CORRECTION

After many years of research that was characterized by evaluation on idiosyncratic and mostly non-public data sets, 2011 saw the creation of the first "Helping Our Own" (HOO) grammatical error correction shared task. The 2011 task was focused on automated writing assistance for writers in the natural language processing community. Dale and Kilgarriff [2010] first proposed the task to the community. They suggested collecting initial data from the ACL anthology with a focus on non-native authors. Papers by non-native writers that were manually identified as containing a sufficient number of errors were then to be annotated and corrected by copy editors and serve as a development set. Dale and Kilgariff, in this initial proposal, expressed optimism that the task would attract enough interest, and in 2011 the first pilot shared task was launched [Dale and Kilgarriff, 2011b].[1]

---

[1]http://clt.mq.edu.au/research/projects/hoo/hoo2011/index.html

9.1.1 THE 2011 HOO TASK

As originally described in Dale and Kilgarriff [2010], the text passages in the 2011 task consisted of samples from 19 papers from the ACL anthology. For each paper, one passage was sampled for development and another for evaluation purposes. The development data contained 1,264 edits/corrections (provided by two professional copy editors), and the test set contained 1,057 edits (provided by one professional copy editor and verified by one of the organizers). Separate files contained the error annotations. The 13 error types that were used were based on the Cambridge University Press Error Coding System [Nicholls, 2003]. The evaluation was based on three criteria: *detection* (identification of an error), *recognition* (identification of the span of an error), and *correction* (identification of at least one correction for the error). For all three criteria, measures of precision, recall, and F-score were calculated.

Six teams participated in the 2011 task. Each team submitted at least one and at most 10 separate runs. The list of teams is shown in Table 9.1:

Table 9.1: HOO 2011 Participating Teams

The range of techniques that were used varied considerably, from purely heuristic approaches in the LI system to mostly data-driven approaches in the UI and NU systems. Different systems also targeted different subsets of errors, making an overall comparison somewhat difficult. Articles and prepositions were targeted by most of the systems due, no doubt, to their prominence in the error statistics of the data set. Overall, the data-driven UI system outperformed all other systems by a sizable margin on F-scores for detection, recognition, and correction, followed by the NU system. The UT system did best on preposition errors, using an n-gram frequency approach. Instead of using a web-corpus as approximated by result counts from the Yahoo! search engine as in Elghafari et al. [2010], they used the ACL anthology itself as the corpus to derive n-gram statistics for the appropriate use of prepositions. Interestingly, Rozovskaya et al. [2012]

also observe that their article and preposition correction modules benefited greatly from adapting to the HOO domain. They achieved this adaptation by incorporating prior probabilities on errors observed in the development data, along the lines of their previous work described in Rozovskaya and Roth [2010b] and Rozovskaya and Roth [2010c] discussed in Chapter 5.

We believe that two tentative conclusions can be drawn from the results in the 2011 pilot shared task. First, as has been the tendency in previous research, data-driven models tend to perform well on article and preposition errors. Second, adaptation to the domain by either incorporating priors on specific error instances or by using a domain corpus as a model for correct preposition usage contributes considerably to the success of the best systems.

9.1.2   THE 2012 HOO TASK

In 2012, the HOO task[2] shifted to a new data set, made available by Cambridge University Press. The set consists of 1,244 annotated exam scripts of English learners taking the First Certificate in English (*CLC-FCE*) exam [Yannakoudakis et al., 2011]. For the 2012 task, the focus was solely on article and preposition errors. All other errors were present in the data, but not annotated. Evaluation scores, as in 2011, were based on detection, recognition, and correction measures, on each of six separate error/correction categories: wrong preposition/article choice (replacement), missing preposition/article (insertion), unwanted preposition/article (deletion). Final scores were computed as standard precision, recall, and F-scores. One thousand of the texts were used for training; 100 additional texts were made available by Cambridge University Press for testing. Since closer inspection revealed some problems in the *CLC* data annotations, participating teams could request changes in the annotation which were adjudicated by the organizers.

The number of participating teams in the 2012 task increased sharply to a total of 14. Table 9.2 lists the participating teams and the references for more detailed information about the systems. Compared to 2011, the participating teams used fewer heuristic methods, and all teams used at least some data-driven technology. Another change from 2011 was the prevalent use of either language models (five systems) or web *n*-gram information (five systems) as part of the data-driven methodology. In addition, a majority of the systems used lexical, part of speech, and chunk features as features for their statistical classifiers, with the most popular classifers being Maximum Entropy and Naïve Bayes. Eight of the 14 systems used the FCE training data as provided, but other data sets were also employed, such as the Google 1TB *n*-gram corpus (5 teams), the *BNC* (3 teams) among others.

The UI and NU systems performed best, with the NU system on top for article errors (according to F-score across detection, recognition, and correction). The UI system produced the best F-scores on preposition detection and recognition tasks, while NU was in first place for preposition correction. Both systems had introduced novel methods compared to their 2011 submission. NU used confidence-weighted learning [Drezde et al., 2008] with language model post-filtering, i.e., eliminating all correction candidates that do not increase the language model score. As in

---

Table 9.2: HOO 2012 Participating Teams

2011, UI added artificially created errors into the training data, according to the confusion matrix observed in the original error data. In 2012 they also used a combination of two classifiers for preposition errors: one is an Averaged Perceptron algorithm, trained on data "inflated" with artificial errors, the other is a Naïve Bayes classifier that directly incorporates prior probabilities of individual confusion pairs (based on the work in Rozovskaya and Roth [2011]). Rozovskaya et al. [2012] provide further discussion of error "inflation" which improves classification performance significantly for both article and preposition errors.

The UD team took a different approach to the competition and used it as an opportunity to develop a flexible and modular framework for error correction in which researchers could add and customize components, tailor features, and experiment with different classifiers.

9.1.3 THE CONLL 2013 SHARED TASK

Table 9.3: CoNLL 2013 Shared Task Participating Teams

The 2013 shared task [Ng et al., 2013][3] took place in conjunction with the Conference on Computational Natural Language Learning (CoNLL).[4] This has garnered for the field of grammatical error correction more publicity and exposure within NLP as CoNLL typically hosts the premier shared task each year. Unlike HOO 2012, which focused solely on article (ArtorDet) and preposition (Prep) errors, this shared task expanded the scope to include three more error types: noun number (NN), verb form (Vform), and subject-verb agreement (SVA) errors. The *NUCLE* v2.3 corpus [Dahlmeier et al., 2013] was used for training and 50 additional essays were annotated for testing. *NUCLE* is a collection of essays written by college-aged, non-native speakers of English attending the National University of Singapore. It should be noted that the essays for the test set were drawn from a different population of students and there was a much higher error rate in the test set than in the training set. This may have had some impact on results for teams which used statistical methods heavily biased by the distribution found in the training data. Precision, recall, and F-score on the test data were calculated using the MaxMatch Scorer [Dahlmeier and Ng, 2012b].

Seventeen teams took part in the competition, making it the largest of three grammatical error correction shared tasks. The team names and affiliations can be found in Table 9.3. Only a handful of the teams that participated in HOO 2012 took part in this one. Many of the teams used a collection of approaches but the primary ones revolved around statistical classification, language modeling, machine translation, and heuristic rules. In addition, many teams used methodologies specific to each error type. Features used in the classification approaches were mostly standard ones: usually a collection of lexical, part of speech, parse, and lemma features. The top performing system was from the UIUC team [Rozovskaya et al., 2013], which extended its previous HOO 2012 submission to address the three new error types. Their overall error correction system performed at an F-score of 31.20 F-score, which bested the next best team's (NTHU) F-score of 25.01.

Table 9.4 shows the top performing team for each error type. The UIUC system outperformed all other systems on each error type except for prepositions, where NARA was the top performer. That system used a maximum entropy classifier with lexical, part-of-speech tags, parse and semantic features. A genetic algorithm was used to filter out noisy features. One interesting aspect of this work was that instead of training on the full range of 36 prepositions found in the corpus, the NARA system focused on the seven most frequently occurring in the *NUCLE* corpus. The UIUC ArtorDet module focused on article errors exclusively and used an Averaged Perceptron classifier trained on the NUCLE training corpus as well as artificial errors, and it was augmented with a language model feature. The noun and two verb error types were tackled by UIUC by use of individual Naïve Bayes models trained on the Google corpus with differing feature sets and candidate selection methods.

---

[3]http://www.comp.nus.edu.sg/~nlp/conll13st.html
[4]There will be a second edition also on grammatical error correction co-located with CoNLL 2014.

Table 9.4: CoNLL 2013 Shared Task Best Performing Systems by Error Type

9.1.4 SUMMARY

The three shared tasks have helped the field considerably in terms of providing corpora and evaluation scripts for future research, as well as baseline performance numbers to compare against. However, several important issues remain. One of the major issues that arose in all the competitions was annotation quality, for both training and test corpora. In all three shared tasks, participating teams found inconsistencies or errors in the training data, but fortunately these errors could then be fixed. Problems with the evaluation corpus were harder to resolve. The HOO 2012 and CoNLL shared tasks handled this by reporting two evaluations: one where performance numbers were based solely on what was originally annotated, and a second one where judgments by the systems which did not mesh with the original annotations could be accounted for pending a vetting procedure by the organizers. In the second case, participants noted instances where the annotations left out alternative valid corrections or the original annotations were incorrect. For all systems, the F-scores increased in the second evaluation, but it is not clear how much of this change was due to the added alternative corrections and how much to the correction of errors in the original annotation. These vetting procedures potentially improve the quality of both the training and evaluation corpora, but they put a strain on the time and resources of the organizers.

Another issue is how to handle multiple errors in the context. The last two shared tasks focused on a subset of the typical learner errors, however as we have seen in earlier chapters, learner errors do not occur in isolation and there may be multiple ways of correcting adjacent errors. Whether or not to correct a preposition, for example, is impacted by whether other errors were corrected, and how they were corrected.

9.2 MACHINE TRANSLATION AND ERROR CORRECTION

Machine translation (MT) has been both an application for article correction and a methodology for preposition and article correction. In the 1990's, it became clear that when machine translation is from languages such as Japanese or Russian into English, the generation of articles becomes a challenge because there is no corresponding word in the source language. Researchers turned to article correction to improve MT output. Murata and Nagao [1993] and Bond et al. [1994], for example, constructed sets of sophisticated rules to predict the count/mass noun status and referential properties of Japanese nouns before translating into English, so that this additional information could be used by the English generation component in the translation system in order to produce the correct article choice. Gawronska-Werngren [1990] worked within a Russian-to-Swedish machine translation system to identify the proper definiteness characteristics of Russian noun phrases, which are not marked for definiteness. The information was then used to generate the correct definiteness markers in Swedish. Heine [1998] used rules to predict definiteness of Japanese noun phrases based on cues from the syntactic environment of the noun phrases in transcribed scheduling dialogs. Once definiteness/indefiniteness was established by these rules, it could be realized as a definite or indefinite article on the English side of the MT system. Knight and Chander [1994] developed a system that they envisioned to be useful in post-editing machine-translated documents. Unlike the earlier approaches, they used a data-driven method and trained their system on the target language (English) with the goal of identifying places where a definite or indefinite article should be inserted to improve the fluency of the MT output. For each of the 1,600 most frequent head nouns in their training corpus, they trained a decision tree on vectors of binary features extracted from the corpus, and then they used the trees to decide which article should be selected for each noun phrase in their test corpus.

Machine translation as a methodology for error correction can be divided into two types: (1) the Noisy Channel Model, in which the task of error correction is framed as the translation of a disfluent sentence into a fluent sentence and (2) Round-Trip Machine Translation, in which an MT system is used in a "black box" manner to correct errors.

9.2.1 NOISY CHANNEL MODEL

In more recent research, MT algorithms themselves have been used to tackle the article and preposition correction problem. MT algorithms automatically translate text from a source language to a target language. Similar algorithms have been employed to create paraphrases of sentences in a single language as well. Brockett et al. [2006] investigated the use of MT techniques to correct learner errors. They used a statistical machine translation (SMT) system to "translate" from "English with errors" to "English without errors," focusing specifically on mass noun errors (such as *many informations*). Their work was motivated by the fact that many learner errors are often not found in isolation, but rather occur within a context where there are several errors and several possible corrections for them. Thus, a focused method would fail on these cases. For example, *And I knew many informations about Christmas...* is best changed by making several corrections, thus transforming the passage to *And I learned a lot about Christmas....*

An SMT system requires millions of examples of correct usage and incorrect usage for it to learn a translation mapping. While examples of correct usage are plentiful in news texts, parallel examples of incorrect usage are much harder to acquire. To solve this, the authors created parallel training data by introducing artificial mass/count noun errors for 14 nouns that are frequently involved in learner errors. Their system was able to correct 61.8% of mass noun errors from a set of 123. It should be noted that this was only a first exploration of statistical MT techniques for error correction, but given enough training data, such a system could potentially be powerful for detecting and correcting errors that involve more than insertion, deletion, or substitution of single words. For example, statistical machine translation is, in principle, capable of re-ordering words and constituents.

Park and Levy [2011] noted that classification approaches fail when there are multiple errors in the same context. They developed a noisy channel approach to *whole sentence error-correction* which makes use of two models: a probabilistic LM that generates an "error-free" sentence and a noise model that inserts errors into the aforementioned sentence. Using a corpus of sentences written by Korean EFL students, their top system configuration showed modest improvements with respect to BLEU score (a metric commonly used to rate machine translation quality). This work was expanded in West et al. [2011], which made use of bilingual data.

Dahlmeier and Ng [2012a] used SMT to tackle an important shortcoming of all classification approaches, namely that classifiers make independent decisions on multiple errors and multiple error types within a sentence and do not take a "global" approach to improving the sentence. SMT, on the other hand, optimizes the probability of a target sentence as a whole, but incorporating specific error models into an SMT system has not successfully been done. To address this problem, they suggested to incorporate correction hypotheses from various error correction modules and scores from *experts* such as classifiers and language models into a global decoding algorithm (*beam search*) for SMT. The decoder takes all of that information into account in order to globally optimize the score of the whole target (corrected) sentence. An evaluation on the HOO 2011 test set shows best performance compared to the HOO 2011 published results on the F-score for correction.

9.2.2   ROUND TRIP MACHINE TRANSLATION (RTMT)

In their prior work in leveraging the web for error correction, Hermet et al. [2008] found that their web-based monolingual model for error correction failed on cases where the preposition used by the writer was in an idiomatic phrase or where the error was due to some deep semantic L1 interference. To counter this deficiency, they experimented with using a "round-trip" machine translation technique [Hermet and Désilets, 2009] to correct preposition errors in French learner writing. The intuition is that by translating a target phrase into the writer's original language, and then back into the target language (in this case French), one can implicitly make use of the L1 dependencies encoded in the machine translation system. This method treats the MT system as a "black box" and its effectiveness is dependent on the machine translation system's performance. The method overlaps heavily with their 2008 work where a web search query phrase is generated from the context surrounding the preposition and then this query phrase is sent to a machine translation engine (in this case Google Translate) to be translated into the source language and then back into French. A correction is made if the target preposition changed in this round-trip process.

As in their 2008 work, Hermet and Désilets [2009] evaluated the system on 133 sentences where all the preposition errors were manually tagged beforehand, thus their method assumes that error detection is done accurately. The machine translation method performed best at 66.4% accuracy, slightly below the more conventional web-counts approach. However, when they combined the two methods into a hybrid system in which the MT system is used as a backup system if the unilingual system does not have enough data to make a classification, performance rose to 82.1%.

Madnani et al. [2012] expanded on the work of Hermet and Désilets [2009] by showing that the RTMT framework could be used to do whole sentence correction by leveraging multiple pivot languages to translate to and from. Their method was motivated by the observation that relying solely on one pivot language would not correct all of the errors in the sentence, and could even create new ones. With multiple pivot languages, there are multiple corrections to choose from, several of which could actually be good rewrites of a phrase or even the entire sentence. The method works as follows. First the target sentence is round-trip translated using eight pivot languages. The next question is how to choose which translation is correct. Their results showed that it is rarely the case that one pivot language could offer a round-trip translation that corrected all errors in the sentence, but several pivot languages, if combined properly, could. To accomplish this, they align all the translations of the source sentence with a novel alignment algorithm to create a lattice. Next, finding a fluent correction can be reduced to finding the best way to traverse the lattice. They proposed six methods based on language model scores, weighting edge scores, and other factors. They evaluated the approaches on a corpus of 200 ESL sentences and found that a greedy approach to lattice traversal actually performed best, creating a better version of the source sentence in 36% of the cases, where "better" is defined as having fewer errors than the original while preserving the original meaning of the sentence. In 33% of the cases, the approach either did not alter the source sentence or produced an alternative that was no better than the source. In 31%, the approach produced a version of the sentence that was worse than the original.

9.3 REAL-TIME CROWDSOURCING OF GRAMMATICAL ERROR CORRECTION

As we saw in Chapter 8, crowdsourcing is an effective option for quick and cheap error correction, thus providing an annotated corpus for evaluating a system or even training a system. A completely new application of crowdsourcing for automatic text-editing and correction was proposed by Bernstein et al. [2010]. Their Soylent system for proofreading and shortening text is "automated," but it is not based on computational intelligence; it uses crowd-based editing instead. What if, at the push of a button, a writer could enlist a group of editors to help with their writing, in near real-time? Soylent automates this process by crowdsourcing the proofreading and editing task. While this method has not yet been used specifically for correction of errors made by non-native writers, we include it here because of its potential for such applications. Obviously, there are two immediate challenges to overcome: (1) How can reasonable quality be ensured when a crowd of unknown workers is involved? and (2) How can a reasonably qualified crowd be retained that will be able to jump into action at a moment's notice?

Soylent addresses the first problem by splitting the writing assistance task into three sub-tasks: finding a problematic text passage, fixing the problem, and verifying the fix ("Find-Fix-Verify"). Each sub-task is carried out by a different set of crowd workers, and at each step, thresholds on agreement between workers are imposed. Bernstein illustrates how the Find-Fix-Verify technique eliminates problems created by two problematic crowd worker types, the "lazy type" and the "eager beaver type." The former only expends minimal effort to find a single error and leaves it at that, while the latter over-corrects and thus tends to do more damage than good. With the Find-Fix-Verify technique in place, the separation between Find and Fix encourages the "lazy worker" to propose fixes for short passages that he/she might otherwise have skipped. The Verify stage will eliminate drastic rewrites and over-zealous corrections, keeping the "eager beaver types" in check. On a sample of five input texts, Soylent's recall was 67% at 88% precision.

Bernstein et al. [2012] provide a framework to address ensuring worker availability by keeping them on retainer to do the task. This also ensures enough responsiveness by crowd-workers that it becomes practical to use real-time crowdsourcing for a variety of tasks. They show that with these measures it is possible to have crowdsourced tasks tackled by crowd workers within half a second.

9.4 DOES AUTOMATED ERROR FEEDBACK IMPROVE WRITING?

In this section we discuss one important aspect of error detection that has not been addressed by NLP research: the efficacy of automated systems for improving the writing of actual system users.

In Chapter 3, we argued that there is an important and growing need for automated grammatical error detection for language learners. Our implicit assumption, throughout this volume, has been that learners would benefit from the feedback and corrections that such systems could provide. However, in the ELL research literature, there is conflicting evidence about whether language learners benefit from written corrective feedback provided by their teachers about specific grammar and usage errors.

Truscott [1996] reviewed a number of earlier studies and concluded that there was no compelling evidence that teacher-provided error correction led to improved second language writing and that the corrections might actually be doing harm. In the years since, educational researchers have taken Truscott's conclusions as a challenge to demonstrate a positive effect of the type of written corrective feedback that consists of highlighting an error and providing the correct form in an adjacent location, such as above or to the side of the error. Bitchener et al. [2005] looked at the writing of 53 intermediate ESL students who received manually written corrections of their errors involving prepositions, the simple past tense, and the definite article. The students wrote four different essays over a 12-week period. Results showed a positive effect of feedback for past tense and article errors (though not for preposition errors) and only when the correction was coupled with brief conferences between the student and an instructor to discuss the errors. More recent studies have demonstrated benefits even without accompanying oral feedback in the form of student-instructor conferences. For example, Bitchener [2008] found a significant improvement in article usage in the writing of low intermediate ESL learners over a two-month period when they received written corrective feedback on the referential use of *a* for first mention and of *the* for subsequent anaphoric mention of a noun phrase. Similar results have been reported by other researchers [Ellis et al., 2008; Sheen, 2007]. These studies support several conclusions:

1. Even feedback on one or a few error types can be of value to the language learner.

2. The benefits are not limited to revisions of the particular essay in which the feedback was given, but instead can generalize across topics and persist over months.

3. Not all types of errors have shown these benefits, so it may be inappropriate to generalize, for example, from article errors to preposition errors or even, within article errors, from mistakes involving *a/the* referential usage to those that involve omission of an article in an obligatory context (e.g., *the students enjoyed course*).

In the studies cited above, high quality corrective feedback was provided by a human expert. The question remains whether an *automated* system, with its lower precision and recall, is beneficial or harmful to the language learner. Clearly, the best way to address this question is to replicate the studies that have used human corrective feedback, but replace the human expert's output with that of an automated error correction system. Then, by looking over a period of months or years at individual language learners writing on a variety of topics, we should be able to measure the effect of the feedback by comparing their performance to that of a matched no-feedback (control) group. Unfortunately, this research has not yet been done. There have, however, been a few preliminary studies that have looked at the effects of *Criterion* and *ESL Assistant* on writers' performance.

Attali [2004] analyzed 9,000 first-draft and final-version essays written by U.S. junior high and high school students using *Criterion*. The results indicated that, on average, errors were reduced in final submissions of essays for the error types that *Criterion* provided feedback on. However, the Attali study was conducted before article and preposition error detection had been incorporated into *Criterion*, and the overwhelming majority of the writers were native speakers of English. Choi [2010] examined the effect of *Criterion* feedback, teacher feedback, and the combination of *Criterion* plus teacher feedback on the writing of ELL students at three levels of proficiency (beginning, intermediate, and advanced) during a three-week intensive ESL summer course. Overall, the degree of improvement in writing, as measured by the reduction in the number of errors from first draft to final revision, was comparable for the *Criterion* and teacher feedback groups, but performance was best for the combined feedback condition. Results for specific usage errors, such as article and preposition errors, were not analyzed separately.

Lipnevich and Smith [2008] examined the effects of feedback on 463 undergraduate students who each wrote a 500-word essay on motivation as a requirement for a psychology course. The students produced a first draft and then returned a week later to revise what they had written. Depending on the condition to which they had been randomly assigned, when revising they were given either no feedback or detailed feedback generated by *Criterion*. At the time of the study, *Criterion* detected article errors but not preposition errors. As a further manipulation, some students were told that the *Criterion* feedback came from a computer and others were told that it came from a human instructor. Lipnevich and Smith found greater improvement in overall essay grade in both feedback conditions. They concluded that detailed feedback specific to individual work was "strongly related to student improvement in essay scores." As in the Attali study, the great majority of these participants were native speakers of English. Chodorow et al. [2010] re-analyzed Lipnevich and Smith's data by splitting it into native and non-native groups and computing the article error rates in the first draft and final versions of the essays. Overall, they found a higher article error rate for non-native speakers than for native speakers, who made just a few random article errors. When examining how performance changed between first draft and final version, they found a small, but statistically significant, decline in error rate for non-native speakers. There was no change for native speakers, due no doubt to a kind of "floor effect" resulting from their already low error rate.

Of course, not all language learning takes place in the classroom, and not all language use is limited to essay writing. Leacock et al. [2009] and Chodorow et al. [2010] describe the results of a study that analyzed the error correction feedback provided to 578 frequent users of *ESL Assistant* about their email, non-technical documents (e.g., student essays), and technical papers (e.g., conference reports and dissertations). The feedback provided by *ESL Assistant* covered errors related to nouns (including article errors), prepositions, verbs, and adjectives. Leacock et al.'s analysis compared the quality of the system's suggested corrections to the quality of the suggestions that the users actually accepted and incorporated into their writing. Quality was evaluated using three categories: (1) good (the suggested correction fixed the problem in the user's input), (2) neutral (there was no net change, as the input and the suggestion were both correct, or the input contained an error that was correctly diagnosed but the suggestion did not correct it), and (3) bad (the input was correct so the suggestion constituted a false positive). There was at least one error flagged in about half of the nearly 40,000 sentences input by the frequent users. Not every error was examined by the user but, of those that were, in about 40% of the cases the suggestion was accepted. For all four error types (nouns, prepositions, verbs, and adjectives), the proportion of bad suggestions that were accepted was significantly lower than the proportion of bad suggestions offered by the system, and the proportion of good suggestions accepted was higher than the proportion of good suggestions offered by the system. The same was generally true across writing domains as there were fewer false positives among the accepted corrections for all three types of writing, and there were more good suggestions that were accepted for two of the three domains—email and technical writing. These results indicate that users did not blindly accept the system's output but instead were discerning in their choices. The data seem to reflect their greater ability to recognize correct usage, even when they were unable to produce it. Finally, an additional analysis of those neutral cases in which there was an error in the sentence but the system's suggestion was incorrect showed that writers were later more likely to re-submit these sentences in an improved form. This suggests that just identifying the location of an error can be of benefit to the user even when the suggestion is incorrect.

To date, few studies of automated error correction have addressed the difference between short-term and long-term effects, as they primarily deal with error rates in original and revised versions of a given document written over a short period of time. Nagata and Nakatani [2010] is a rare exception as they examined the effects of the quality and amount of error feedback on Japanese students' writing of English essays on ten different topics produced over a period of two months. Errors involving articles and noun number were flagged by a human annotator or by an automatic error detection system whose threshold was set to provide either feedback with higher precision but lower recall or feedback with higher recall but lower precision. A control group received no error feedback. Learning was measured in terms of reduction of error rate for the noun phrases in the students' essays. Results showed that learning was quite similar for the human-supplied feedback and the higher-precision lower-recall automated feedback conditions, and that both were better than the no-feedback condition. By contrast, the higher-recall lower-precision automated feedback condition actually yielded results that were worse than the no-feedback condition. This latter finding lends support to the common assumption in the field of grammatical error detection that it is better to provide less feedback than to provide incorrect feedback and that systems should, therefore, be optimized for precision even though that often means reduced recall.

The scarcity of longitudinal research on the effects of automated error feedback points, perhaps, to a fundamental difference between the goals of those who build automated error correction systems and those who educate language learners. The automated systems operate in the immediacy of the present; they are designed to improve the quality of the current document by finding errors and indicating the changes that need to be made. Educators, on the other hand, seek to improve the quality of the writer by changing that individual's knowledge base which is used to produce new documents. A system that improves documents is not necessarily a system that improves writers. In order to demonstrate the value of automated error correction for education, we must provide controlled, longitudinal studies that can measure the long-term effects of automated error correction on second language writing. Given the number of variables that must be examined, including proficiency level of the second language users, genres of writing, types of errors, and forms of feedback, this is a daunting task, but one that we believe is well worth doing.

CHAPTER 10

Conclusion

In this volume, we have given an overview of the challenges and opportunities in the area of automatic grammatical error detection for learners. In the introduction, we noted that this is an exciting area of research because there is the potential for real impact given the vast number of people learning another language and because there is no shortage of interesting problems that need to be solved. We have seen that the problems facing language learners are linguistically diverse. Depending on the learner's L1, the constructions that are most difficult in the L2 vary. We have also seen that there are identifiable sub-domains of errors that are problematic across learners, and that these error types constitute a sizable number of errors made by learners. This allows us to gain a foothold in establishing methods for their correction by modeling these errors in a specific and targeted way.

Despite the surge in interest and resources since the first edition of this volume, there still is ample room for improvement. For example, only a subset of data-driven algorithms have been examined for their usefulness, and there are many left to investigate. Recent research is beginning to explore other approaches such as leveraging large-scale corpora and machine translation technology. Finally, while an algorithm that could serve as a general error detection and correction mechanism still remains an elusive target, there does not seem to be any fundamental reason why it would be beyond reach. Here we suggest some ideas and directions for future research:

- **Annotation for Evaluation:** Prior to 2010, there were very few data resources and no reasonably sized public data set for evaluation. Since then, there have been several data sets created (such as the *CLC-FCE* and *NUCLE*) and the shared tasks have helped push toward consistent evaluation standards. However, there are still no accepted annotation standards and the shared tasks highlighted the difficulty in maintaining consistent annotations within a corpus. Anyone developing such a standard and an accompanying public, annotated data set would have a major impact on the field, just as in other research areas in natural language processing where unified evaluation criteria and corpora have led to much progress.

- **Error Detection for Underrepresented Languages:** There has been considerable work on detecting errors in ELL writing, but there remains a need to develop similar tools for detecting errors by learners trying to master other languages. As noted in Chapter 7, this is partially due to the lack of NLP tools and large-scale corpora available for those languages. Dickinson et al. [2010] have developed an automated web-scraping method to build a large corpus of Korean texts to train a statistical classifier for detecting omitted postpositional particles [Israel et al., 2013], a direction that might also prove useful for other languages.

- **Research on Other Error Types:** Although articles, prepositions, and collocations are important, there are other high frequency error types that have received far less attention. For example, fragments, run-on sentences, and problems with verb tense and aspect are just a few examples of error types that are common in learner writing.

- **L1-Specific Error Detection Modules:** Another open area of research is the creation of error detection modules that take into account the L1 of the writer. There are methods which attempt to do this automatically [Hermet and Désilets, 2009; Rozovskaya and Roth, 2011; Tetreault and Chodorow, 2009] with some promising results.

- **Collaboration with Second Language Learning and Education Groups:** As mentioned in the previous section, most work in error detection has been conducted in "test tube" fashion: systems are evaluated on internal data sets with the goal of maximizing some evaluation metric. While this is certainly necessary, we also feel that there are many potential benefits of working with others from different research backgrounds related to language education. ELL or education programs at universities can be great sources of learner data, as well as annotated learner data. One type of collaborative project might involve testing an error detection module in a classroom setting and measuring the long-term effects of using such a system on the learners' writing. Another unexplored area is a spoken dialogue tutoring system which could give feedback to the writer on his or her writing quality.

- **Applications of Grammatical Error Correction:** In this volume, we have treated grammatical error detection and correction as an end in itself to provide feedback to language learners. However, high performance grammatical error correction can also be used as a tool for other NLP applications such as automatic essay scoring [Attali and Burstein, 2006] and native language identification [Koppel et al., 2005; Tetreault et al., 2012]. Additionally, many of the methodologies used for language learner grammatical error correction overlap with the methodologies used to rate the quality of machine translation output [Bojar et al., 2013; Callison-Burch et al., 2012].

Despite the many challenges, there continues to be significant interest and progress in the field of automated grammatical error detection and correction. There have been papers on this topic at nearly every major Computational Linguistics conference in the last three years, with ACL 2011 devoting an entire session to error correction. In fact, there have been more papers on grammatical error correction in the last three years than in all the years prior to 2010. Workshops such as the Innovative Use of NLP for Building Educational Applications, which just completed its eighth year, and three shared tasks also bring added exposure to the field. We hope that this volume contributes to the growing interest by encouraging researchers to take a closer look at the field and its many challenging problems.

APPENDIX A

Appendix A: Learner Corpora

This appendix contains all textual learner corpora (keyed-in or transcribed) that we are aware of and that have at least some publicly accessible URL or reference. Many of the URLs give only very sparse information about the availability or makeup of the corpus, so we are not able to provide a consistent level of detail in the following list.

As a supplement, the University Catholique de Louvain maintains an exhaustive list of reported corpora: spoken corpora, corpora that can be searched online but not available in their entirety, and reported corpora that are not publicly available. The URL for Learner Corpora Around the World is `http://www.uclouvain.be/en-cecl-lcworld.html`.

A.1 BASQUE

IRAKAZI: A Basque learner corpus is being collected in a collaboration between several Basque language schools. It consists of the writings of students at different levels of proficiency. Of the 221,000 words in the corpus, more than half have already been annotated for some error types.

Size: 221,000 words

Error-tagged: partially

URL: `http://ixa.si.ehu.es/irakazi`

A.2 ENGLISH

Cambridge Learner Corpus (CLC): CLC is based on Cambridge ESOL English exams administered around the world. It consists of over 200,000 exam texts written by students with 148 different native languages, and is fully annotated for L1, proficiency level, and errors.

Size: 200,000 texts

Error-tagged: yes

URL: `http://www.cambridge.org.br/for-teachers/cambridge-international-corpus?uk_url=/br/elt/catalogue/subject/custom/item3646603/Cambridge-English-Corpus-Cambridge-Learner-Corpus`

Cambridge ESOL First Certificate in English (CLC-FCE): The CLC-FCE corpus is a collection of 1,244 scripts (essays) extracted from the larger CLC. These scripts were written for the Cambridge First Certificate in English examination. Each script includes the score, error annotation, and demographic information such as the writer's L1 and age bracket.

Size: 1,244 texts

Error-tagged: yes
URL: `http://ilexir.co.uk/applications/clc-fce-dataset/`

Chinese Learners of English Corpus (CLEC):   CLEC is constructed from the writing of Chinese learners of English at five proficiency levels which are equally represented in the corpus. The corpus is annotated with 61 different error tags.

Size: 1 million words
Error-tagged: yes
URL: `http://langbank.engl.polyu.edu.hk/corpus/clec.html`

Chungdahm corpus of English: The Chungdahm corpus consists of 131 million words from Korean student essays collected by the Chungdahm Institute, a Korean chain of English language schools.

Size: 131 million words
Error-tagged: yes

English L2—Japanese L1 Learner Corpus: This is a small collection of essays and story retellings produced by Japanese speakers.

Size: small
Error-tagged: no
URL: `http://www.eng.ritsumei.ac.jp/asao/lcorpus/`

English Taiwan Learner Corpus (ETLC):   ETLC is a web-based corpus of writing by English learners in Taiwan, mostly high school and university students.

Size: 5 million words
Error-tagged: partially
URL: `http://lrn.ncu.edu.tw/Teacher%20Web/David%20Wible/The%20English%20TLC.htm`[1]

The Gachon Learner Corpus: This is a corpus of writing by South Korean students.

Size: 3 million words
Error-tagged: no
URL: `http://koreanlearnercorpusblog.blogspot.be/p/corpus.html/`

Hong Kong University of Science and Technology (HKUST) corpus: Writings by university students, mostly assignments from EFL classes and final exams. The corpus contains error annotations.

Size: 30 million words
Error-tagged: yes

---

[1]`http://lrn.ncu.edu.tw/Teacher%20Web/David%20Wible/The%20English%20TLC.htm`

Indianapolis Business Learner Corpus (IBLC):   This corpus contains both EFL and native job application letters and resumes. Subjects are business students from the U.S., Belgium, and Finland.

> Size: unknown
> Error-tagged: no
> URL: `http://www.liberalarts.iupui.edu/icic/research/indianapolis_business_learner_corpus`

Interactive Spoken Language Education corpus of non-native spoken English (ISLE):   ISLE is a corpus of 18 hours of speech from 23 German and 23 Italian learners of English, 12 hours of which are error annotated.

> Size: 18 hours of speech
> Error-tagged: partially
> URL: `http://citeseerx.ist.psu.edu/showciting?cid=1847843`

International Corpus of Learner English (ICLE):   The ICLE corpus [Granger et al., 2002b], one of the first language learner corpora to be developed, contains essays written by English learners from 16 different L1 backgrounds. The learners are advanced-level students of English as a foreign language. Access is granted for academic purposes to participants in the project.

> Size: over 3 million words
> Error-tagged: partially
> Source: Granger et al. [2002b]
> URL: `http://www.uclouvain.be/en-cecl-icle.html`

Janus Pannonius University Learner Corpus: This corpus of essays and research papers was collected from Hungarian students writing in English.

> Size: 221 texts
> Error-tagged: no
> URL: `http://joeandco.blogspot.com/`

Japanese English as a Foreign Language Learner Corpus (JEFLL):   This corpus is mostly based on the writing of English learners from Japanese secondary schools. The corpus is currently still under development and not yet released.

> Size: 700,000 million words
> Error-tagged: yes
> URL: `http://jefll.corpuscobo.net/`

Learner Business Letters Corpus: This corpus of business letters written by Japanese native speakers is a subset of the Online Business Letter Corpus. It is not clear if it is available separately from the larger corpus.

> Size: 1,020,060 words
> Error-tagged: no

URL: http://www.someya-net.com/concordancer/index.html

Asao Kojiro's Learner Corpus Data: This is a corpus of essays written by Japanese college students.

> Size: 123 essays
> Error-tagged: no
> URL: http://www.eng.ritsumei.ac.jp/asao/lcorpus/

Longman Learners' Corpus (LLC):   LLC is a corpus of English written by learners from a wide variety of L1 backgrounds and proficiency levels. The corpus is available commercially.

> Size: 10 million words
> Error-tagged: no
> URL: http://www.pearsonlongman.com/dictionaries/corpus/learners.html

Montclair Electronic Language Database (MELD):   Student writing. Error annotation is not based on a set of fixed annotation categories but instead uses the error string and the correction *error/correction* in place of error tags.

> Size: 44,477 words annotated; 53,826 words unannotated
> Error-tagged: partially
> URL: http://www.chss.montclair.edu/linguistics/MELD/

Multimedia Adult English Learner Corpus (MAELC):   MAELC contains audio and video recordings, and a database of teacher logs, student work samples and classroom materials collected at The Portland State University.

> Size: unknown
> Error-tagged: no
> URL: http://www.labschool.pdx.edu/research/methods/maelc/intro.html

National Institute of Information and Communications Technology Japanese Learner English corpus (NICT-JLE, or SST):   The NICT-JLE corpus comprises two million words of transcribed speech data from Japanese learners of English. The data were transcribed from 1,281 speech samples of an oral proficiency interview (Standard Speaking Test, SST). The proficiency level of each speaker is part of the information available in the corpus. The corpus is tagged for morphological, grammatical, and lexical errors; the tag set comprises 46 different tags.

> Size: 1.2 million words
> Error-tagged: yes
> Source: Izumi et al. [2004b] and Izumi et al. [2004c]
> URL: http://alaginrc.nict.go.jp/nict_jle/index_E.html

National University of Singapore Corpus of Learner English (NUCLE):   1,400 English learner essays on many different topics, more than one million words, fully error-annotated.

> Size: 1+ million words

Error-Tagged: yes
URL: http://r2m.nus.edu.sg/cos/o.x?c=/r2m/license_product&ptid=5730&func=viewProd&pid=28

Polish Learner English Corpus: The text in this corpus was collected at the Universities of Lodz and Lancaster as part of the Polish and English Language Corpora for Research and Application (PELCRA) project. The project is ongoing and error annotation is planned.
Size: 500,000 words
Error-tagged: planned
URL: http://pelcra.pl/res/

SILS Learner Corpus of English: Collected at the School of International Liberal Studies at Waseda University in Japan, this corpus is a collection of student essays.
Size: unknown
Error-tagged: no
URL: http://www.f.waseda.jp/vicky/learner/index.html

Singapore Corpus of Research in Education (SCoRE): SCoRE is a corpus of classroom interactions, teaching materials, and student artifacts from Singapore schools. It is focused on discourse and does not contain error annotations, but it is richly annotated with respect to discourse and semantics.
Size: unknown
Error-tagged: no
URL: http://www.nie.edu.sg/research-projects/singapore-corpus-research-education-score

Teachers of English Language Education Centre Secondary Learner corpus (TSLC or TeleNex Student Corpus): Writings of Hong Kong students at secondary level. The corpus is not error-annotated.
Size: 2 million words
Error-tagged: no
Source: Allan [2002]
URL: http://www.telenex.hku.hk/telec/smain/sintro/intro.htm

Thai English Learner Corpus (TELC): TELC consists of university entrance exams and undergraduate writing.
Size: 1.5 million words
Error-tagged: no
URL: http://ling.arts.chula.ac.th/TLE/index.html

University of Illinois at Urbana-Champaign ESL Error Annotation   Learner corpus with error-annotated sentences for a subset of ICLE and CLEC sentences. Annotations are by native speakers of English.

>   Size: 55,000 words of ICLE sentences; 10,000 words of CLEC sentences
>   Error-tagged: yes
>   Source: Rozovskaya and Roth [2010a]
>   URL: `http://cogcomp.cs.illinois.edu/page/resources/ESL%20error%20annot`
`ation`

Written Corpus of Learner English (WRICLE):   This is a corpus of essays written in English by Spanish university students in the Department of English at the Universidad Autonoma de Madrid.

>   Size: 750,000 words
>   Error-tagged: no
>   URL: `http://www.uam.es/proyectosinv/woslac/Wricle/`

Uppsala Student English Corpus (USE):   The corpus contains 1,489 essays written by Swedish university students of English and is available for non-commercial use.

>   Size: 1.2 million words
>   Error-tagged: no
>   URL: `http://www.engelska.uu.se/Forskning/engelsk_sprakvetenskap/Forskn`
`ingsomraden/Electronic_Resource_Projects/USE-Corpus/`

Vienna-Oxford International Corpus of English (VOICE):   This corpus consists of recordings and transcriptions of naturally occurring face-to-face interactions in English as a lingua franca. The corpus currently contains the equivalent of about 120 hours of recorded speech.

>   Size: 1 million words
>   Error-tagged: no
>   URL: `http://www.univie.ac.at/voice/`

A.3   FINNISH

International Corpus of Learner Finnish (ICLFI):   ICLFI is currently still under development. It consists of student artifacts from a wide range of international universities where Finnish is taught.

>   Size: 265,000 words (in 2008)
>   Error-tagged: no
>   URL: `http://metashare.csc.fi/repository/browse/international-corpus-`
`of-learner-finnish-iclfi/632aa08efccc11e18b49005056be118e2d2ce40d2a224c85b`
`4602c9d1337b876/`

A.4   FRENCH

French Learner Language Oral Corpora (FLLOC):   FLLOC consists of sound files, transcripts, and morphosyntactically tagged transcripts. It is available for research purposes.
> Size: 4,000 files
> Error-tagged: no
> URL: http://www.flloc.soton.ac.uk/

A.5   GERMAN

EAGLE: An Error-Annotated Corpus of Beginning Learner German: EAGLE is an annotated corpus of learner German, collected at Ohio State University.
> Size: 81 essays
> Error-tagged: yes
> URL: http://www.researchgate.net/publication/220746623_EAGLE_an_Error-Annotated_Corpus_of_Beginning_Learner_German

Fehlerannotiertes Lernerkorpus des Deutschen als Fremdsprache (FALKO):   FALKO is an annotated corpus of learner German, collected at the Humboldt University Berlin and still under development.
> Size: 280,000 words
> Error-tagged: yes
> URL: http://www.linguistik.hu-berlin.de/institut/professuren/korpuslinguistik/forschung/falko

A.6   SPANISH

Corpus Escrito del Espanol L2 (CEDEL2):   Collected at the Universidad Autonoma de Madrid and Universidad de Granada, the corpus consists of writings of native English speakers in Spanish. The goal is to collect a total of 1 million words.
> Size: 700,000 words
> Error-tagged: no
> URL: http://www.uam.es/proyectosinv/woslac/collaborating.htm

French Interlanguage Database (FRIDA):   The data in FRIDA were collected by the Centre for English Corpus Linguistics (CECL), which also produces and maintains the ICLE corpus.
> Size: 450,000 words
> Error-tagged: partially
> URL: http://sites.uclouvain.be/cecl/projects/Frida/fridatext.htm

A.7 MULTIPLE LANGUAGES

Multilingual Corpus for Teaching and Translation (COMET): English, Spanish, and German learner data.

  Size: unknown
  Error-tagged: no
  URL: `http://www.fflch.usp.br/dlm/comet/`

Bibliography

Mohammad Said Al-Zahrani. *Knowledge of English lexical collocations among male Saudi college students majoring in English at a Saudi University.* PhD thesis, Indiana University of Pennsylvania, Pennsylvania. 27

Md. Jahangir Alam, Naushad UzZaman, and Mumit Khan. *N*-gram based statistical checker for Bangla and English. In *Proceedings of International Conference on Computer and Information Technology (ICCIT)*, 2006. 84

Itziar Aldabe, Bertol Arrieta, Arantza Díaz de Ilarraza, Montse Maritxalar, Maite Oronoz, Larriatz Uria, and Leire Amoros. Learner and error corpora based computational systems. *Corpora and ICT in Language Studies: PALC 2005*, 13, 2007. 91

Keith Allan. Nouns and countability. *Language*, 56(3):541–567, September 1980. DOI: 10.2307/414449. 26

Quentin Grant Allan. The TELEC secondary learner corpus: A resource for teacher development. In S. Granger, J. Hung, and S. Petch-Tyson, editors, *Computer Learner Corpora, Second Language Acquisition and Foreign Language Teaching*, pages 195–211. John Benjamins, Amsterdan, 2002. DOI: 10.1075/lllt.6. 119

Øistein E. Andersen. Semi-automatic ESOL error annotation. *English Profile Journal*, 2, September 2011. DOI: 10.1017/S2041536211000018. 90, 91

Rie Kubota Ando, Tong Zhang, and Peter Bartlett. A framework for learning predictive structures from multiple tasks and unlabeled data. *Journal of Machine Learning Research*, 6:1817–1853, 2005. 55

Antti Arppe. Developing a grammar checker for Swedish. In *Proceedings of the Twelfth Nordic Conference in Computational Linguistics (NoDaLiDa)*, pages 13–27, Trondheim, Norway, 2000. 7, 78

Yigal Attali. Exploring the feedback and revision features of *Criterion*. In *Proceedings of the Annual Meeting of the National Council on Measurement in Education*, pages 1–22, San Diego, CA, 2004. 110

Yigal Attali and Jill Burstein. Automated essay scoring with e-rater® v. 2. *The Journal of Technology, Learning and Assessment*, 4(3), 2006. 114

Eric Steven Atwell. How to detect grammatical errors in a text without parsing it. In *Proceedings of the Third Conference of the European Association for Computational Linguistics (EACL)*, pages 38–45, Copenhagen, 1987. DOI: 10.3115/976858.976865. 15

Jens Bahns and Moira Eldaw. Should we teach EFL students collocations? *System*, 21(1):101–114, February 1993. DOI: 10.1016/0346-251X(93)90010-E. 27

Emily M. Bender, Dan Flickinger, Stephan Oepen, and Timothy Baldwin. Arboretum: Using a precision grammar for grammar checking in CALL. In *Proceedings of the Integrating Speech Technology in Learning/Intelligent Computer Assisted Language Learning (inSTIL/ICALL) Symposium: NLP and Speech Technologies in Advanced Language Learning Systems*, Venice, 2004. 7, 8, 78, 83

Morton Benson, Evelyn Benson, and Robert Ilson. *The BBI Dictionary of Combinatory English Words*. John Benjamins, Philadelphia, revised edition, 1997. 65

Gabor Berend, Veronika Vincze, Sina Zarrieß, and Richárd Farkas. LFG-based features for noun number and article grammatical errors. In *Proceedings of the Seventeenth Conference on Computational Natural Language Learning: Shared Task*, pages 62–67, Sofia, Bulgaria, August 2013. Association for Computational Linguistics. URL http://www.aclweb.org/anthology/W13-3608.

Taylor Berg-Kirkpatrick, David Burkett, and Dan Klein. An empirical investigation of statistical significance in NLP. In *EMNLP-CoNLL*, pages 995–1005, 2012. 43

Shane Bergsma, Dekang Lin, and Randy Goebel. Web-scale *n*-gram models for lexical disambiguation. In *Proceedings of the 21st International Joint Conference on Artifical Intelligence*, pages 1507–1512, Pasadena, 2009. 57

Michael S. Bernstein, Greg Little, Robert C. Miller, Björn Hartmann, Mark S. Ackerman, David R. Karger, David Crowell, and Katrina Panovich. Soylent: a word processor with a crowd inside. In *UIST*, pages 313–322, 2010. DOI: 10.1145/1866029.1866078. 108

Michael S. Bernstein, David R. Karger, Robert C. Miller, and Joel Brandt. Analytic methods for optimizing realtime crowdsourcing. *CoRR*, abs/1204.2995, 2012. 109

Yves Bestgen and Sylviane Granger. Categorizing spelling errors to assess L2 writing. *International Journal of Continuing Engineering Education and Life-Long Learning (IJCEELL)*, 21 (2/3):235–252, 2011. DOI: 10.1504/IJCEELL.2011.040201. 81

Pinaki Bhaskar, Aniruddha Ghosh, Santanu Pal, and Sivaji Bandyopadhyay. May I check the English of your paper!!! In *Proceedings of the Generation Challenges Session at the 13th European Workshop on Natural Language Generation*, pages 250–253, Nancy, France, September 2011. Association for Computational Linguistics. URL http://www.aclweb.org/anthology/W11-2839.

Pinaki Bhaskar, Aniruddha Ghosh, Santanu Pal, and Sivaji Bandyopadhyay. Detection and correction of preposition and determiner errors in English: HOO 2012. In *Proceedings of the Seventh Workshop on Building Educational Applications Using NLP*, pages 201–207, Montréal, Canada, June 2012. Association for Computational Linguistics. URL http://www.aclweb.org/anthology/W12-2023.

Juhani Birn. Detecting grammar errors with Lingsoft's Swedish grammar checker. In *Proceedings of the Twelfth Nordic Conference in Computational Linguistics (NoDaLiDa)*, pages 28–40, Trondheim, Norway, 2000. 78

John Bitchener. Evidence in support of corrective feedback. *Journal of Second Language Writing*, 17:102–118, 2008. DOI: 10.1016/j.jslw.2007.11.004. 110

John Bitchener, Stuart Young, and Denise Cameron. The effect of different types of corrective feedback on ESL student writing. *Journal of Second Language Writing*, 14:191–205, 2005. DOI: 10.1016/j.jslw.2005.08.001. 22, 109

Phil Blunsom and Timothy Baldwin. Multilingual deep lexical acquisition for HPSGs via supertagging. In *Proceedings of the 2006 Conference on Empirical Methods in Natural Language Processing (EMNLP)*, pages 164–171, Sydney, July 2006. DOI: 10.3115/1610075.1610101. 7

Ondřej Bojar, Christian Buck, Chris Callison-Burch, Christian Federmann, Barry Haddow, Philipp Koehn, Christof Monz, Matt Post, Radu Soricut, and Lucia Specia. Findings of the 2013 Workshop on Statistical Machine Translation. In *Proceedings of the Eighth Workshop on Statistical Machine Translation*, pages 1–44, Sofia, Bulgaria, August 2013. Association for Computational Linguistics. URL http://www.aclweb.org/anthology/W13-2201. 114

Philip Bolt. An evaluation of grammar-checking programs as self-help learning aids for learners of English as a Foreign Language. *Computer Assisted Language Learning*, 5(1):49–91, 1992. DOI: 10.1080/0958822920050106. 9

Francis Bond, Kentaro Ogura, and Satoru Ikehara. Countability and number in Japanese-to-English machine translation. In *Proceedings of the 15th International Conference on Computational Linguistics (COLING)*, pages 32–38, 1994. DOI: 10.3115/991886.991889. 105

Gerlof Bouma. Collocation extraction beyond the independence assumption. In *Proceedings of the ACL 2010 Conference Short Papers*, ACLShort '10, pages 109–114, Stroudsburg, PA, USA, 2010. Association for Computational Linguistics. URL http://dl.acm.org/citation.cfm?id=1858842.1858862. 69

Adriane Boyd and Detmar Meurers. Data-driven correction of function words in non-native English. In *Proceedings of the Generation Challenges Session at the 13th European Workshop on Natural Language Generation*, pages 267–269, Nancy, France, September 2011. Association for Computational Linguistics. URL http://www.aclweb.org/anthology/W11-2844. 57

Adriane Boyd, Marion Zepf, and Detmar Meurers. Informing determiner and preposition error correction with hierarchical word clustering. In *Proceedings of the Seventh Workshop on Building Educational Applications Using NLP*, pages 208–215, Montréal, Canada, June 2012. Association for Computational Linguistics. URL http://www.aclweb.org/anthology/W12-2024.

Thorsten Brants and Alex Franz. Web 1T 5-gram version 1, 2006. Available at http://www.ldc.upenn.edu/Catalog/CatalogEntry.jsp?catalogId=LDC2006T13. 50

Chris Brockett, William B. Dolan, and Michael Gamon. Correcting ESL errors using phrasal SMT techniques. In *Proceedings of the 21st International Conference on Computational Linguistics (COLING) and 44th Annual Meeting of the Association for Computational Linguistics (ACL)*, pages 249–256, Sydney, 2006. 51, 79, 106

Jill Burstein, Martin Chodorow, and Claudia Leacock. Automated essay evaluation: The Criterion Online Writing Service. *AI Magazine*, 25(3):27–36, 2004. 21, 60

Miriam Butt, Helge Dyvik, Tracy Holloway King, Hiroshi Masuichi, and Christian Rohrer. The parallel grammar project. In *Proceedings of the 19th International Conference on Computational Linguistics (COLING) 2002 Workshop on Grammar Engineering and Evaluation*, pages 1–7, Taipei,Taiwan, 2002. 7

Jan Buys and Brink van der Merwe. A tree transducer model for grammatical error correction. In *Proceedings of the Seventeenth Conference on Computational Natural Language Learning: Shared Task*, pages 43–51, Sofia, Bulgaria, August 2013. Association for Computational Linguistics. URL http://www.aclweb.org/anthology/W13-3606.

Donna K. Byron. The uncommon denominator: A proposal for consistent reporting of pronoun resolution results. *Computational Linguistics*, 27(4), 2001. DOI: 10.1162/089120101753342671. 44

Aoife Cahill, Martin Chodorow, Susanne Wolff, and Nitin Madnani. Detecting missing hyphens in learner text. In *Proceedings of the Eighth Workshop on Innovative Use of NLP for Building Educational Applications*, pages 300–305, Atlanta, Georgia, June 2013a. Association for Computational Linguistics. URL http://www.aclweb.org/anthology/W13-1739. 82

Aoife Cahill, Nitin Madnani, Joel Tetreault, and Diane Napolitano. Robust systems for preposition error correction using Wikipedia revisions. In *Proceedings of the 2013 Conference of the North American Chapter of the Association for Computational Linguistics: Human Language Technologies*, Atlanta, GA, USA, June 2013b. Association for Computational Linguistics. 43, 53, 55, 97, 98

Chris Callison-Burch. Fast, cheap, and creative: Evaluating translation quality using Amazon's Mechanical Turk. In *Proceedings of the 2009 Conference on Empirical Methods in*

Natural Language Processing (EMNLP), pages 286–295, Singapore, August 2009. DOI: 10.3115/1699510.1699548. 95, 97

Chris Callison-Burch, Philipp Koehn, Christof Monz, Matt Post, Radu Soricut, and Lucia Specia. Findings of the 2012 workshop on statistical machine translation. In *Proceedings of the Seventh Workshop on Statistical Machine Translation*, pages 10–51, Montréal, Canada, June 2012. Association for Computational Linguistics. URL http://www.aclweb.org/anthology/W 12-3102. 114

Andrew A. Carlson, Jeffrey Rosen, and Dan Roth. Scaling up context-sensitive text correction. In *Proceedings of the 13th Conference on Innovative Applications of Artificial Intelligence*, pages 45–50, 2001. 81

Mark Catt and Graeme Hirst. An intelligent CALL system for grammatical error diagnosis. *Computer Aided Language Learning*, 3:3–26, 1990. DOI: 10.1080/0958822900030102. 8, 9

Yu-Chia Chang, Jason S. Chang, Hao-Jan Chen, and Hsien-Chin Liou. An automatic collocation writing assistant for Taiwanese EFL learners: A case of corpus-based NLP technology. *Computer Assisted Language Learning*, 21(3):283–299, 2008. DOI: 10.1080/09588220802090337. 73, 74

Eugene Charniak. Tree-bank grammars. In *Proceedings of the 13th National Conference on Artificial Intelligence*, pages 1031–1036, 1996. 7

Eugene Charniak. Immediate head-parsing for language models. In *Proceedings of the 39th Annual Meeting of the Association for Computational Linguistics*, pages 124–131, 2001. DOI: 10.3115/1073012.1073029. 56

Martin Chodorow and Claudia Leacock. An unsupervised method for detecting grammatical errors. In *Proceedings of the Conference of the North American Chapter of the Association of Computational Linguistics (NAACL)*, pages 140–147, 2000. 76, 93

Martin Chodorow, Joel Tetreault, and Na-Rae Han. Detection of grammatical errors involving prepositions. In *Proceedings of the Fourth ACL-SIGSEM Workshop on Prepositions*, pages 25–30, 2007. DOI: 10.3115/1654629.1654635. 55

Martin Chodorow, Michael Gamon, and Joel Tetreault. The utility of grammatical error detection systems for English language learners: Feedback and assessment. *Language Testing*, 27(3):335–353, July 2010. DOI: 10.1177/0265532210364391. 111

Martin Chodorow, Markus Dickinson, Ross Israel, and Joel Tetreault. Problems in evaluating grammatical error detection systems. In *Proceedings of COLING 2012*, pages 611–628, Mumbai, India, December 2012. The COLING 2012 Organizing Committee. URL http://www.aclweb.org/anthology/C12-1038. 33, 35, 36

Jaeho Choi. The use of feedback in the ESL writing class integrating automated essay scoring. In *Proceedings of the Society for Information Technology and Teacher Education International Conference (SITE)*, pages 3008–3012, San Diego, 2010. 110

Noam Chomsky. Remarks on nominalization. In R. A. Jacobs and P. S. Rosenbaum, editors, *Readings in English Transformational Grammar*, pages 184–221. Ginn and Company, Waltham, MA, 1970. 24

Kenneth Church and Patrick Hanks. Word association norms, mutual information, and lexicography. *Computational Linguistics*, 16(1):22–29, 1990. 66, 71

Kenneth Church, William Gale, Patrick Hanks, and Donald Hindle. Using statistics in lexical analysis. In Uri Zernik, editor, *Lexical Acquisition: Exploiting On-line Resources to Build a Lexicon*, pages 115–164. Lawrence Erlbaum, Hillsdale, New Jersey, 1991. 66

Jacob Cohen. A coefficient of agreement for nominal scales. *Educational and Psychological Measurement*, 20(1):37–46, 1960. DOI: 10.1177/001316446002000104. 34

Robert J. Connors and Andrea A. Lunsford. Frequency of formal errors in current college writing, or Ma and Pa Kettle do research. *College Composition and Communication*, 39(4):395–409, 1988. DOI: 10.2307/357695. 17, 19

Ann Copestake and Dan Flickinger. An open source grammar development environment and broad coverage English grammar using HPSG. In *Proceedings of the Second Conference on Language Resources and Evaluation (LREC)*, pages 591–600, 2000. 7

Anthony Paul Cowie. Multiword units in newspaper language. In S. Granger, editor, *Perspectives on the English Lexicon*, pages 101–116. Cahiers de l'Institut de Linguistique de Louvain, Louvain-la-Neuve, 1991. 27

Anthony Paul Cowie. Multi-word lexical units and communicative language teaching. In P. Arnaud and H. Bejoint, editors, *Vocabulary and Applied Linguistics*, pages 1–12. Macmillan, London, 1992. 27

Ido Dagan and Sean Engelson. Committee-based sampling for training probabilistic classifiers. In *Proceedings of the Twelfth International Conference on Machine Learning (ICML)*, pages 150–157, 1995. 93

Estelle Dagneaux, Sharon Denness, Sylviane Granger, and Fanny Meunier. Error tagging manual, Version 1.1, 1996. 92

Daniel Dahlmeier and Hwee Tou Ng. Grammatical error correction with Alternating Structure Optimization. In *Proceedings of the 49th Annual Meeting of the Association for Computational Linguistics: Human Language Technologies*, pages 915–923, Portland, Oregon, USA, June

2011a. Association for Computational Linguistics. URL http://www.aclweb.org/antholo
gy/P11-1092. 41, 49, 53, 55

Daniel Dahlmeier and Hwee Tou Ng. Correcting semantic collocation errors with L1-induced
paraphrases. In *Proceedings of the 2011 Conference on Empirical Methods in Natural Language
Processing*, pages 107–117, Edinburgh, Scotland, UK., July 2011b. Association for Computational Linguistics. URL http://www.aclweb.org/anthology/D11-1010. 74

Daniel Dahlmeier and Hwee Tou Ng. A beam-search decoder for grammatical error correction.
In *Proceedings of the 2012 Joint Conference on Empirical Methods in Natural Language Processing
and Computational Natural Language Learning*, pages 568–578, Jeju Island, Korea, July 2012a.
Association for Computational Linguistics. URL http://www.aclweb.org/anthology/D
12-1052. 82, 107

Daniel Dahlmeier and Hwee Tou Ng. Better evaluation for grammatical error correction. In *Proceedings of the 2012 Conference of the North American Chapter of the Association for Computational
Linguistics: Human Language Technologies*, pages 568–572, Montréal, Canada, June 2012b. Association for Computational Linguistics. URL http://www.aclweb.org/anthology/N12-
1067. 36, 104

Daniel Dahlmeier, Hwee Tou Ng, and Thanh Phu Tran. NUS at the HOO 2011 pilot shared
task. In *Proceedings of the Generation Challenges Session at the 13th European Workshop on Natural Language Generation*, pages 257–259, Nancy, France, September 2011. Association for
Computational Linguistics. URL http://www.aclweb.org/anthology/W11-2841.

Daniel Dahlmeier, Hwee Tou Ng, and Eric Jun Feng Ng. NUS at the HOO 2012 shared task.
In *Proceedings of the Seventh Workshop on Building Educational Applications Using NLP*, pages
216–224, Montréal, Canada, June 2012. Association for Computational Linguistics. URL
http://www.aclweb.org/anthology/W12-2025.

Daniel Dahlmeier, Hwee Tou Ng, and Siew Mei Wu. Building a large annotated corpus of
learner english: The NUS corpus of learner english. In *Proceedings of the Eighth Workshop on
Innovative Use of NLP for Building Educational Applications*, pages 22–31, Atlanta, Georgia,
June 2013. Association for Computational Linguistics. URL http://www.aclweb.org/ant
hology/W13-1703. 19, 22, 91, 92, 104

Robert Dale and Adam Kilgarriff. Helping Our Own: Text massaging for computational linguistics as a new shared task. In *Sixth International Natural Language Generation Conference*,
Trim, Co. Meath, Ireland, July 2010. 99, 100

Robert Dale and Adam Kilgarriff. Helping Our Own: The HOO 2011 pilot shared task. In *Proc.
of ENLG*, 2011a. 31, 36, 42

Robert Dale and Adam Kilgarriff. Helping Our Own: The HOO 2011 pilot shared task. In *Proceedings of the Generation Challenges Session at the 13th European Workshop on Natural Language Generation*, pages 242–249, Nancy, France, September 2011b. Association for Computational Linguistics. URL http://www.aclweb.org/anthology/W11-2838. 80, 99

Robert Dale, Ilya Anisimoff, and George Narroway. HOO 2012: A report on the preposition and determiner error correction shared task. In *Proceedings of the Seventh Workshop on Building Educational Applications Using NLP*, pages 54–62, Montréal, Canada, June 2012. Association for Computational Linguistics. URL http://www.aclweb.org/anthology/W12-2006. 31, 36, 89

Gerard M. Dalgish. Computer-assisted ESL research and courseware development. *Computers and Composition*, 2(4):45–61, 1985. 22

Vidas Daudaravicius. VTEX determiner and preposition correction system for the HOO 2012 shared task. In *Proceedings of the Seventh Workshop on Building Educational Applications Using NLP*, pages 225–232, Montréal, Canada, June 2012. Association for Computational Linguistics. URL http://www.aclweb.org/anthology/W12-2026.

Rachele De Felice and Stephen G. Pulman. A classifier-based approach to preposition and determiner error correction in L2 English. In *Proceedings of the 22nd International Conference on Computational Linguistics (COLING)*, pages 169–176, Manchester, UK, 2008. DOI: 10.3115/1599081.1599103. 31, 55

Rachele De Felice and Stephen G. Pulman. Automatic detection of preposition errors in learner writing. *CALICO Journal*, 26(3):512–528, 2009. 41, 50

Arantza Díaz De Ilarraza, Koldo Gojenola, and Maite Oronoz. Detecting erroneous uses of complex postpositions in an agglutinative language. In *Proceedings of the 22nd International Conference on Computational Linguistics (COLING)*, pages 31–34, Manchester, UK, 2008. 79

Paul Deane. A nonparametric method for extraction of candidate phrasal terms. In *Proceedings of the 43rd Annual Meeting of the Association for Computational Linguistics (ACL)*, pages 605–613, Ann Arbor, MI, 2005. DOI: 10.3115/1219840.1219915. 69, 70, 72

Nuwar Diab. The transfer of Arabic in the English writings of Lebanese students. *The ESPeccialist*, 18(1):71–83, 1997. 22, 23

Ana Diaz-Negrillo and Jesus Fernández-Dominguez. Error tagging systems for learner corpora. *Revista Española de Lingüística Aplicada (RESLA)*, 19:83–102, 2006. 92

Markus Dickinson, Ross Israel, and Sun-Hee Lee. Building a korean web corpus for analyzing learner language. In *Proceedings of the NAACL HLT 2010 Sixth Web as Corpus Workshop*, pages 8–16, NAACL-HLT, Los Angeles, June 2010. Association for Computational Linguistics. URL http://www.aclweb.org/anthology/W10-1502. 113

Luca Dini and Giovanni Malnati. Weak constraints and preference rules. In P. Bennett and P. Paggio, editors, *Preference in Eurotra*, pages 75–90. Commission of the European Communities, Luxembourg, 1993. 8

William B. Dolan, Stephen D. Richardson, and Lucy Vanderwende. Automatically deriving structured knowledge bases from on-line dictionaries. Technical Report MSR-TR-93-07, Microsoft Research, May 1993. 10

Richard Domeji, Ola Knutsson, Johan Carlberger, and Viggo Kann. Granska – an efficient hybrid system for Swedish grammar checking. In *Proceedings of the Twelfth Nordic Conference in Computational Linguistics (NoDaLiDa)*, pages 49–56, Trondheim, Norway, 2000. 78

Steven Donahue. Formal errors: Mainstream and ESL students. Presented at the 2001 Conference of the Two-Year College Association (TYCA), 2001. 17

Shona Douglas and Robert Dale. Towards robust PATR. In *Proceedings of the 15th International Conference on Computational Linguistics (COLING)*, pages 468–474, Nantes, France, 1992. DOI: 10.3115/992133.992143. 8

Mark Drezde, Koby Crammer, and Fernando Pereira. Confidence-weighted linear classification. In *Proceedings of the 25th International Conference on Machine Learning*, pages 184–191, Helsinki, Finland, 2008. DOI: 10.1145/1390156.1390190. 101

Ted Dunning. Accurate methods for the statistics of surprise and coincidence. *Computational Linguistics*, 19(1):61–74, 1993. 66, 68

Jens Eeg-Olofsson and Ola Knuttson. Automatic grammar checking for second language learners–the of prepositions. In *Proceedings of the 14th Nordic Conference in Computational Linguistics (NoDaLiDa)*, 2003. 78

B. Efron and R. Tibshirani. *An Introduction to the Bootstrap*. Chapman and Hall/CRC Monographs on Statistics and Applied Probability Series. Chapman & Hall, 1993. ISBN 9780412042317. URL http://books.google.com/books?id=gLlpIUxRntoC. DOI: 10.1007/978-1-4899-4541-9. 43

Anas Elghafari, Detmar Meurers, and Holger Wunsch. Exploring the data-driven prediction of prepositions in English. In *Coling 2010: Posters*, pages 267–275, Beijing, China, August 2010. Coling 2010 Organizing Committee. URL http://www.aclweb.org/anthology/C 10-2031. 57, 100

Rob Ellis, Younghee Sheen, Mihoko Murakami, and Hide Takashima. The effects of focused and unfocused written corrective feedback in an English as a foreign language context. *System*, 36:353–371, 2008. DOI: 10.1016/j.system.2008.02.001. 110

Sean Engelson and Ido Dagan. Minimizing manual annotation cost in supervised training from corpora. In *Proceedings of the 34th Meeting of the Association for Computational Linguistics (ACL)*, pages 319–326, 1996. DOI: 10.3115/981863.981905. 93

Stefan Evert. *The Statistics of Word Cooccurrences: Word Pairs and Collocations.* PhD thesis, Institut für maschinelle Sprachverarbeitung, University of Stuttgart, Stuttgart, 2004. 66, 69

Stefan Evert and Brigitte Krenn. Methods for the qualitative evaluation of lexical association measures. In *Proceedings of the 39th Annual Meeting of the Association for Computational Linguistics (ACL)*, pages 188–195, Toulouse, 2001. 69

Stefan Evert and Brigitte Krenn. Using small random samples for the manual evaluation of statistical association measures. *Computer Speech and Language*, 19(4):450–466, 2005. DOI: 10.1016/j.csl.2005.02.005. 69

Daniel Fallman. The *penguin*: Using the web as a database for descriptive and dynamic grammar and spell checking. In *Proceedings of the Conference on Human Factors in Computing Systems (CHI)*, pages 616–617, Minneapolis, Minnesota, 2002. DOI: 10.1145/506443.506511. 57

Mohammed Farghal and Hussein Obiedat. Collocations: A neglected variable in EFL. *International Review of Applied Linguistics in Language Teaching*, 33(4):315–331, 1995. DOI: 10.1515/iral.1995.33.4.315. 27

Tom Fawcett. An introduction to roc analysis. *Pattern Recogn. Lett.*, 27(8):861–874, June 2006. ISSN 0167-8655. URL http://dx.doi.org/10.1016/j.patrec.2005.10.010. DOI: 10.1016/j.patrec.2005.10.010. 35

John R. Firth. *Modes of Meaning.* Oxford University Press, Oxford, 1957. 65

Joseph Fleiss. *Statistical Methods for Rates and Proportions.* John Wiley, New York, second edition, 1981. 42

Dan Flickinger and Jiye Yu. Toward more precision in correction of grammatical errors. In *Proceedings of the Seventeenth Conference on Computational Natural Language Learning: Shared Task*, pages 68–73, Sofia, Bulgaria, August 2013. Association for Computational Linguistics. URL http://www.aclweb.org/anthology/W13-3609.

Gerhard Fliedner. A system for checking NP agreement in German texts. In *Proceedings of the Student Research Workshop at the 40th Annual Meeting of the Association for Computational Linguistics (ACL)*, pages 12–17, Philadelphia, 2002. 78

Michael Flor and Yoko Futagi. On using context for automatic correction of non-word misspellings in student essays. In *Proceedings of the Seventh Workshop on Innovative use of NLP for Educational Applications Using NLP (BEA)*, pages 105–115, 2012. 81

Michael Flor and Yoko Futagi. Producing an annotated corpus with automatic spelling correction. In S. Granger, G. Gilquin, and F. Meunier (eds.). *Twenty Years of Learner Corpus Research: Looking back, Moving ahead*. Corpora and Language in Use—Proceedings 1, Louvain-la-Neuve: Presses universitaires de Louvain, 139–154. 2013. 81

Jennifer Foster and Øistein Andersen. GenERRate: Generating errors for use in grammatical error detection. In *Proceedings of the Fourth Workshop on Building Educational Applications Using NLP (BEA)*, pages 82–90, 2009. 52

Frederik Fouvry. Constraint relaxation with weighted feature structures. In *Proceedings of the Eighth International Workshop on Parsing Technologies (IWPT-03)*, Nancy, France, 2003. 8

Annette Frank, Tracy Holloway King, Jonas Kuhn, and John Maxwell. Optimality theory style constraint ranking in large scale LFG grammars. In *Proceedings of the Lexical Functional Grammar Conference (LFG) LFG-98*, Brisbane, 1998. 7

Ian S. Fraser and Lynda M. Hodson. Twenty-one kicks at the grammar horse. *English Journal*, 67(9):49–54, December 1978. DOI: 10.2307/815131. 2

Yoko Futagi, Paul Deane, Martin Chodorow, and Joel Tetreault. A computational approach to detecting collocation errors in the writing of non-native speakers of English. *Computer Assisted Language Learning*, 21:353–367, 2008. DOI: 10.1080/09588220802343561. 28, 72

William Gale, Ken Church, and David Yarowsky. Work on statistical methods for word sense disambiguation. In *Proceedings of the AAAI Fall Symposium on Probabilistic Approaches to Natural Language*, pages 54–60, Cambridge, MA, 1992. DOI: 10.3115/981344.981378. 13

Michael Gamon. Using mostly native data to correct errors in learners' writing. In *Proceedings of the Eleventh Annual Conference of the North American Chapter of the Association for Computational Linguistics (NAACL)*, Los Angeles, 2010. 40, 41, 53, 55, 56, 63

Michael Gamon. High-order sequence modeling for language learner error detection. In *Proceedings of the Sixth Workshop on Innovative Use of NLP for Building Educational Applications*, pages 180–189, Portland, Oregon, June 2011. Association for Computational Linguistics. URL http://www.aclweb.org/anthology/W11-1422. 79, 84

Michael Gamon, Carmen Lozano, Jessie Pinkham, and Tom Reutter. Practical experience with grammar sharing in multilingual NLP. Technical Report MSR-TR-93-16, Microsoft Research, 1997. 10

Michael Gamon, Jianfeng Gao, Chris Brockett, Alex Klementiev, William B. Dolan, Dmitriy Belenko, and Lucy Vanderwende. Using contextual speller techniques and language modeling for ESL error correction. In *Proceedings of the International Joint Conference on Natural Language Processing (IJCNLP)*, pages 449–456, Hyderabad, India, 2008. 31, 38, 39, 50, 55, 60, 90

134 BIBLIOGRAPHY

Michael Gamon, Claudia Leacock, Chris Brockett, William B. Dolan, Jianfeng Gao, Dmitriy Belenko, and Alexandre Klementiev. Using statistical techniques and web search to correct ESL errors. *CALICO Journal*, 26(3), 2009. 15, 75, 76, 77

Barbara Gawronska-Werngren. "Translation great problem" - on the problem of inserting articles when translating from Russian into Swedish. In *Proceedings of the 13th International Conference on Computational Linguistics (COLING)*, pages 133–138, 1990. DOI: 10.3115/997939.997962. 106

Mandeep Singh Gill and Gurpreet Singh Lehal. A grammar checking system for Punjabi. In *Proceedings of the 22nd International Conference on Computational Linguistics (COLING)*, pages 149–152, 2008. 78

Andrew Golding. A Bayesian hybrid method for context sensitive spelling correction. In *Proceedings of the Third Workshop on Very Large Corpora (WVLC-3)*, pages 39–53, 1995. 14, 81

Andrew Golding and Dan Roth. Applying Winnow to context-sensitive spelling correction. In *Proceedings of the International Conference on Machine Learning (ICML)*, pages 182–190, 1996. 14, 81

David Graff and Christopher Cieri. English Gigaword, 2003. Available at http://www.ldc.upenn.edu/Catalog/CatalogEntry.jsp?catalogId=LDC2003T05. 50

Sylviane Granger. The International Corpus of Learner English: A new resource for foreigh language learning and teaching and second language acquisition research. *TESOL Quarterly*, 37(3):538–546, 2003. DOI: 10.2307/3588404. 91

Sylviane Granger, Estelle Dagneaux, and Fanny Meunier. *The International Corpus of Learner English: Handbook and CD-ROM*. Presses Universitaires de Louvain, Louvain-la-Neuve, 2002b. 92, 117

Yan Guo and Gulbahar H. Beckett. The hegemony of English as a global language: Reclaiming local knowledge and culture in China. *Convergence*, 40(1-2):117–132, 2007. 3

Kirl L. Hagen. Unification-based parsing applications for intelligent foreign language tutoring systems. *Calico Journal*, 2(2):2–8, 1995. 8

Na-Rae Han, Martin Chodorow, and Claudia Leacock. Detecting errors in English article usage with a maximum entropy classifier trained on a large, diverse corpus. In *Proceedings of the Fourth International Conference on Language Resources and Evaluation (LREC)*, pages 1625–1628, Lisbon, Portugal, 2004. 55, 89

Na-Rae Han, Martin Chodorow, and Claudia Leacock. Detecting errors in English article usage by non-native speakers. *Natural Language Engineering*, 12(2):115–129, 2006. DOI: 10.1017/S1351324906004190. 40, 49, 55

Na-Rae Han, Joel Tetreault, Soo-Hwa Lee, and Jin-Young Ha. Using an error-annotated learner corpus to develop an ESL/EFL error correction system. In *Proceedings of the Seventh International Conference on Language Resources and Evaluation (LREC)*, Malta, 2010. 52, 53

George E. Heidorn. Augmented phrase structure grammars. In B.L. Webber and R. Schank, editors, *Theoretical Issues in Natural Language Processing*, pages 1–5. Association for Computational Linguistics, 1975. 10

George E. Heidorn. Intelligent writing assistance. In R. Dale, H. Moisl, and H. Somers, editors, *Handbook of Natural Language Processing*, pages 181–207. Marcel Dekker, New York, 2000. 10, 83

George E. Heidorn, Karen Jensen, Lance A. Miller, Roy J. Byrd, and Martin Chodorow. The *Epistle* text-critiquing system. *IBM Systems Journal*, 21(3):305–326, 1982. DOI: 10.1147/sj.213.0305. 7, 10

Trude Heift and Mathias Schulze. *Errors and Intelligence in Computer-Assissted Language Learning: Parsers and Pedagogues*. Routledge, New York and London, 2007. 2, 4, 9, 80

Michael Heilman, Aoife Cahill, and Joel Tetreault. Precision isn't everything: A hybrid approach to grammatical error detection. In *Proceedings of the Seventh Workshop on Building Educational Applications Using NLP*, pages 233–241, Montréal, Canada, June 2012. Association for Computational Linguistics. URL http://www.aclweb.org/anthology/W12-2027.

Julia E. Heine. Definiteness predictions for Japanese noun phrases. In *Proceedings of the 36th Annual Meeting of the Association for Computational Linguistics (ACL) and 17th International Conference on Computational Linguistics (COLING)*, pages 519–525, Montreal, 1998. DOI: 10.3115/980845.980932. 106

Johannes Heinecke, Jurgen Kunze, Wolfgang Menzel, and Idno Schroder. Eliminative parsing with graded constraints. In *Proceedings of the 36th Annual Meeting of the Association for Computational Linguistics (ACL) and 17th International Conference on Computational Linguistics (COLING)*, pages 243–259, 1998. DOI: 10.3115/980845.980933. 8

Antje Helfrich and Bradley Music. Design and evaluation of grammar checkers in multiple languages. In *Proceedings of the 18th International Conference on Computational Linguistics (COLING)*, pages 1036–1040, 2000. DOI: 10.3115/992730.992800. 11

Matthieu Hermet and Alain Désilets. Using first and second language models to correct preposition errors in second language authoring. In *Proceedings of the Fourth Workshop on Building Educational Applications Using NLP (BEA)*, pages 64–72, 2009. 57, 107, 108, 114

Matthieu Hermet, Alain Désilets, and Stan Szpakowicz. Using the web as a linguistic resource to automatically correct lexico-syntactic errors. In *Proceedings of the Sixth International Conference on Language Resources and Evaluation (LREC)*, pages 390–396, Marrekech, Morocco, 2008. 57, 58, 59, 107

Jimmie Hill. Revising priorities: From grammatical failure to collocational success. In Michael Lewis, editor, *Teaching Collocation*, pages 47–70. Language Teaching Publications, London, 2000. 28

Graeme Hirst and Alexander Budanitsky. Correcting real-world spelling errors by restoring lexical cohesion. *Natural Language Engineering*, 11(1):87–111, March 2005. DOI: 10.1017/S1351324904003560. 80

Peter Howarth. The phraseology of learners' academic writing. In A.P. Cowie, editor, *Phraseology: Theory, Analysis, and Application*, pages 161–186. Clarendon Press, Oxford, 1998. 27

Jeng-Yih Hsu. Lexical collocations and their impact on the online writing of Taiwanese college English majors and non-English major. *Electronic Journal of Foreign Language Teaching*, 4(2): 192–209, 2007. 27

Kenji Imamura, Kuniko Saito, Kugatsu Sadamitsu, and Hitoshi Nishikawa. Grammar error correction using pseudo-error sentences and domain adaptation. In *Proceedings of the 50th Annual Meeting of the Association for Computational Linguistics (Volume 2: Short Papers)*, pages 388–392, Jeju Island, Korea, July 2012. Association for Computational Linguistics. URL http://www.aclweb.org/anthology/P12-2076. 52

Diana Zaiu Inkpen and Graeme Hirst. Acquiring collocations for lexical choice between near-synonyms. In *Unsupervised Lexical Acquisition: Proceedings of the Workshop of the ACL Special Interest Group on the Lexicon (SIGLEX)*, pages 67–76, Philadelphia, 2002. DOI: 10.3115/1118627.1118636. 69

Aminul Islam and Diane Inkpen. Real-word spelling correction using Google Web 1T 3-grams. In *Proceedings of the Conference on Empirical Methods in Natural Language Processing (EMNLP)*, pages 1241–1249, Singapore, 2009. 81

Ross Israel, Joel Tetreault, and Martin Chodorow. Correcting comma errors in learner essays, and restoring commas in newswire text. In *Proceedings of the 2012 Conference of the North American Chapter of the Association for Computational Linguistics: Human Language Technologies*, pages 284–294, Montréal, Canada, June 2012. Association for Computational Linguistics. URL http://www.aclweb.org/anthology/N12-1029. 82

Ross Israel, Markus Dickinson, and Sun-Hee Lee. Detecting and correcting learner korean particle omission errors. In *Proceedings of the Sixth International Joint Conference on Natural Language Processing*, pages 1419–1427, Nagoya, Japan, October 2013. Asian Federation of Natural Language Processing. URL http://www.aclweb.org/anthology/I13-1199. 113

Elitza Ivanova, Delphine Bernhard, and Cyril Grouin. Handling outlandish occurrences: Using rules and lexicons for correcting NLP articles. In *Proceedings of the Generation Challenges Session at the 13th European Workshop on Natural Language Generation*, pages 254–256, Nancy, France, September 2011. Association for Computational Linguistics. URL http://www.aclweb.o rg/anthology/W11-2840.

Emi Izumi, Kiyotaka Uchimoto, Toyomi Saiga, Thepchai Supnithi, and Hitoshi Isahara. Automatic error detection in the Japanese learners' English spoken data. In *Companion Volume to the Proceedings of the 41st Annual Meeting of the Association for Computational Linguistics (ACL)*, pages 145–148, 2003. DOI: 10.3115/1075178.1075202. 22, 51, 53, 54, 55

Emi Izumi, Kiyotaka Uchimoto, and Hitoshi Isahara. The overview of the SST speech corpus of Japanese learner English and evaluation through the experiment on automatic detection of learners' errors. In *Proceedings of Language Resource and Evaluation Conference (LREC) 2004*, pages 1435–1438, Lisbon, Portugal, 2004a. 41

Emi Izumi, Kiyotaka Uchimoto, and Hitoshi Isahara. The NICT JLE Corpus: Exploiting the language learners' speech database for research and education. *International Journal of the Computer, the Internet and Management*, 12(2):119–125, 2004b. 118

Emi Izumi, Kiyotaka Uchimoto, and Hitoshi Isahara. SST speech corpus of Japanese learners' English and automatic detection of learners' errors. *International Computer Archive of Modern English Journal*, 28:31–48, 2004c. 54, 55, 118

Carl James. *Errors in Language Learning and Use: Exploring Error Analysis*. Addison Wesley Longman, 1998. 17, 21, 32

Karen Jensen, George E. Heidorn, Lance A. Miller, and Yael Ravin. Parse fitting and prose fixing: Getting a hold on ill-formedness. *American Journal of Computational Linguistics*, 9(3–4):147–160, 1983. 9, 10

Karen Jensen, George E. Heidorn, and Stephen D. Richardson. *Natural Language Processing: The PLNLP Approach*. Kluwer, Dordrecht, 1993. DOI: 10.1007/978-1-4615-3170-8. 10

Zhongye Jia, Peilu Wang, and Hai Zhao. Grammatical error correction as multiclass classification with single model. In *Proceedings of the Seventeenth Conference on Computational Natural Language Learning: Shared Task*, pages 74–81, Sofia, Bulgaria, August 2013. Association for Computational Linguistics. URL http://www.aclweb.org/anthology/W13-3610.

Jia-Yan Jian, Yu-Chia Chang, and Jason S. Chang. Collocational translation memory extraction based on statistical and linguistic information. Presented at ROCLING 2004, Conference on Computational Linguistics and Speech Processing, 2004. 73

Janne Bondi Johannessen, Kristin Hagen, and Pia Lane. The performance of a grammar checker with deviant language input. In *Proceedings of the 19th International Conference on Computational Linguistics (COLING)*, pages 1–8, Taipei, Taiwan, 2002. DOI: 10.3115/1071884.1071894. 7

Daniel Jurafsky and James H. Martin. *Speech and Language Processing*. Prentice Hall, 2 Edition, 2008. 4, 56

John S. Justeson and Slava M. Katz. Technical terminology: Some linguistic properties and an algorithm for identification in text. *Natural Language Engineering*, 1(1):9–27, 1995. DOI: 10.1017/S1351324900000048. 66

Ting-hui Kao, Yu-wei Chang, Hsun-wen Chiu, Tzu-Hsi Yen, Joanne Boisson, Jian-cheng Wu, and Jason S. Chang. CoNLL-2013 shared task: Grammatical error correction nthu system description. In *Proceedings of the Seventeenth Conference on Computational Natural Language Learning: Shared Task*, pages 20–25, Sofia, Bulgaria, August 2013. Association for Computational Linguistics. URL http://www.aclweb.org/anthology/W13-3603.

Fred Karlsson, Atro Voutilainen, Juha Heikkil a, and Arto Anttila. *Constraint Grammar: A Language-Independent System for Parsing Unrestricted Text*. Mouton de Gruyter, Berlin and New York, 1995. DOI: 10.1515/9783110882629. 7, 78

Adam Kilgarriff. Googleology is bad science. *Computational Linguistics*, 33(1):147–151, 2007. DOI: 10.1162/coli.2007.33.1.147. 59

Kevin Knight and Ishwar Chander. Automated postediting of documents. In *Proceedings of the Twelfth National Conference on Artificial Intelligence (AAAI)*, pages 779–784, Seattle, 1994. 14, 54, 106

Ekaterina Kochmar, Øistein Andersen, and Ted Briscoe. HOO 2012 error recognition and correction shared task: Cambridge University submission report. In *Proceedings of the Seventh Workshop on Building Educational Applications Using NLP*, pages 242–250, Montréal, Canada, June 2012. Association for Computational Linguistics. URL http://www.aclweb.org/anthology/W12-2028.

Moshe Koppel, Jonathan Schler, and Kfir Zigdon. Determining an author's native language by mining a text for errors. In *Proceedings of the eleventh ACM SIGKDD international conference on Knowledge discovery in data mining*, pages 624–628, Chicago, IL, 2005. ACM. DOI: 10.1145/1081870.1081947. 114

Brigitte Krenn and Stefan Evert. Can we do better than frequency? A case study on extracting PP-verb collocations. In *Proceedings of the Workshop on Collocations at the 50th Annual Meeting of the Association for Computational Linguistics (ACL)*, pages 36–46, Toulouse, 2001. 69

Karen Kukich. Techniques for automatically correcting words in text. *Computing Surveys*, 24(4): 377–439, 1992. DOI: 10.1145/146370.146380. 80

Anoop Kunchukuttan, Ritesh Shah, and Pushpak Bhattacharyya. IITB system for CoNLL 2013 shared task: A hybrid approach to grammatical error correction. In *Proceedings of the Seventeenth Conference on Computational Natural Language Learning: Shared Task*, pages 82–87, Sofia, Bulgaria, August 2013. Association for Computational Linguistics. URL http://www.aclweb.org/anthology/W13-3611.

Stan C. Kwasny and Norman K. Sondheimer. Relaxation theories for parsing ill-formed input. *American Journal of Computational Linguistics*, 7:99–108, 1981. 8

Richard J. Landis and Gary G. Koch. The measurement of observer agreement for categorical data. *Biometrics*, 33:159–174, 1977. DOI: 10.2307/2529310. 34

Claudia Leacock and Martin Chodorow. Automated grammatical error detection. In M.D. Shermis and J.C. Burstein, editors, *Automated Essay Scoring: A Cross-Disciplinary Perspective*, pages 195–207. Lawrence Erlbaum Associates, Mahwah, NJ, 2003. 21, 76

Claudia Leacock, Michael Gamon, and Chris Brockett. User input and interactions on Microsoft Research ESL Assistant. In *Proceedings of the Fourth Workshop on Building Educational Applications Using NLP (BEA)*, pages 73–81, 2009. 111

Chong Min Lee, Soojeong Eom, and Markus Dickinson. Towards analyzing Korean learner particles. In *Proceedings of the Workshop on Automatic Analysis of Learner Language (AALL) at CALICO 2009*, Tempe, AZ, 2009a. 78

Jieun Lee, Jung-Tae Lee, and Hae-Chang Rim. Korea University system in the HOO 2012 shared task. In *Proceedings of the Seventh Workshop on Building Educational Applications Using NLP*, pages 251–256, Montréal, Canada, June 2012. Association for Computational Linguistics. URL http://www.aclweb.org/anthology/W12-2029.

John Lee. Automatic article restoration. In *Proceedings of the Human Language Technology Conference of the North American Chapter of the Association for Computational Linguistics (HLT)*, pages 31–36, Boston, 2004. DOI: 10.3115/1614038.1614044. 54

John Lee and Stephanie Seneff. Automatic grammar correction for second-language learners. In *Proceedings of the Ninth International Conference on Spoken Language Processing (Interspeech)*, pages 1978–1981, 2006. 56

John Lee and Stephanie Seneff. Correcting misuse of verb forms. In *Proceedings of the 46th Annual Meeting of the Association for Computational Linguistics: Human Language Technology (ACL/HLT)*, pages 174–182, 2008. 41, 51, 79

John Lee, Ming Zhou, and Xiaohua Lin. Detection of non-native sentences using machine-translated training data. In *Proceedings of the Annual Conference of the North American Chapter of the Association for Computational Linguistics (NAACL)*, pages 93–97, 2007. 83

John Lee, Joel Tetreault, and Martin Chodorow. Human evaluation of article and noun number usage: Influences of context and construction variability. In *Proceedings of the Third Linguistic Annotation Workshop (LAW)*, pages 60–63, Suntec, Singapore, 2009b. 87, 89

Beth Levin. *English Verb Classes and Alternations: A Preliminary Investigation.* University of Chicago Press, Chicago, 1993. 24

Dekang Lin. An information-theoretic definition of similarity. In *In Proceedings of the 15th International Conference on Machine Learning(ICML-98)*, pages 296–304, Madison, Wisconsin, 1998. 71

Dekang Lin. Automatic identification of non-compositional phrases. In *Proceedings of the 37th Annual Meeting of the Association for Computational Linguistics (ACL)*, pages 317–324, 1999. DOI: 10.3115/1034678.1034730. 71

Anastasiya A. Lipnevich and Jeffrey K. Smith. Response to assessment feedback: The effects of differential feedback on students' performance. Technical report, Educational Testing Service, 2008. 110

Ann Li-E Liu. A corpus-based lexical semantic investigation of verb-noun miscollocations in Taiwan learners English. Master's thesis, Tamkang University, Taipei, 2002. 28, 73

Ann Li-E Liu, David Wible, and Nai-Lung Tsao. Automated suggestions for miscollocations. In *Proceedings of the ACL Fourth Workshop on Innovative Use of NLP for Building Educational Applications (BEA)*, pages 47–50, Boulder, Colorado, June 2009. 73

Xiaohua Liu, Bo Han, Kuan Li, Stephan Hyeonjun Stiller, and Ming Zhou. SRL-based verb selection for ESL. In *Proceedings of the 2010 Conference on Empirical Methods in Natural Language Processing*, pages 1068–1076, Cambridge, MA, October 2010. Association for Computational Linguistics. URL http://www.aclweb.org/anthology/D10-1104. 79

Anke Lüdeling, Maik Walter, Emil Kroymann, and Peter Adolphs. Multilevel error annotation in learner corpora. In *Proceedings of the Corpus Linguistics Conference*, Birmingham, United Kingdom, 2005. 88

Gerard Lynch, Erwan Moreau, and Carl Vogel. A Naïve Bayes classifier for automatic correction of preposition and determiner errors in ESL text. In *Proceedings of the Seventh Workshop on Building Educational Applications Using NLP*, pages 257–262, Montréal, Canada, June 2012. Association for Computational Linguistics. URL http://www.aclweb.org/anthology/W 12-2030.

Nina H. MacDonald, Lawrence T. Frase, Patricia S. Gingrich, and Stacey A. Keenan. The Writer's Workbench: Computer aids for text analysis. *IEEE Transactions on Communications*, 30(1), 1982. DOI: 10.1109/TCOM.1982.1095380. 7

Nitin Madnani, Martin Chodorow, Joel Tetreault, and Alla Rozovskaya. They can help: Using crowdsourcing to improve the evaluation of grammatical error detection systems. In *Proceedings of the 49th Annual Meeting of the Association for Computational Linguistics: Human Language Technologies*, pages 508–513, Portland, Oregon, USA, June 2011. Association for Computational Linguistics. URL http://www.aclweb.org/anthology/P11-2089. 42, 95, 97

Nitin Madnani, Joel Tetreault, and Martin Chodorow. Exploring grammatical error correction with not-so-crummy machine translation. In *Proceedings of the Seventh Workshop on Building Educational Applications Using NLP*, pages 44–53, Montréal, Canada, June 2012. Association for Computational Linguistics. URL http://www.aclweb.org/anthology/W12-2005. 108

David M. Magerman. Statistical decision-tree models for parsing. In *Proceedings of the 33rd Annual Meeting of the Association for Computational Linguistics (ACL)*, pages 276–283, 1995. DOI: 10.3115/981658.981695. 7

Christopher D. Manning and Hinrich Schütze. *Foundations of Statistical Natural Language Processing*. MIT Press, 1999. 4, 66, 67, 68, 69

Mitchell P. Marcus, Beatrice Santorini, and Mary Ann Marcinkiewicz. Building a large annotated corpus of English: The Penn Treebank. *Computational Linguistics*, 19:313–330, 1993. 7

Aurélien Max and Guillaume Wisniewski. Mining naturally-occurring corrections and paraphrases from Wikipedia's revision history. In *Proceedings of LREC*, 2010. URL http://perso.limsi.fr/amax/Max_10a_LREC.pdf. 97

Chris S. Mellish. Some chart-based techniques for parsing ill-formed input. In *Proceedings of the 27th Annual Meeting of the Association for Computational Linguistics (ACL)*, pages 102–109, 1989. DOI: 10.3115/981623.981636. 9

Igor Mel'čuk. Lexical Functions: A Tool for the Description of Lexical Relations in the Lexicon. In Leo Wanner, editor, *Lexical functions in lexicography and natural language processing*, pages 37–102. John Benjamins, Philadelphia, 1996. DOI: 10.1075/slcs.31. 66

Wolfgang Menzel. Error diagnosing and selection in a training system for second language learning. In *Proceedings of the 13th International Conference on Computational Linguistics (COLING)*, pages 422–424, Helsinki, 1990. 8

George A. Miller. WordNet: A lexical database for English. *Communications of the ACM*, 38 (11):39–41, 1995. DOI: 10.1145/219717.219748. 49

Guido Minnen, Francis Bond, and Ann Copestake. Memory-based learning for article generation. In *Proceedings of the Conference on Natural Language Learning (CoNLL)*, pages 43–48, 2000. DOI: 10.3115/1117601.1117611. 54

Tom M. Mitchell. *Machine Learning*. McGraw-Hill, 1997. 4

Roger Mitton and T. Okada. The adaptation of an English spellchecker for Japanese writers. In *Symposium on Second Language Writing*, Nagoya, Japan, September 2007. URL http://eprints.bbk.ac.uk/592/. 81

Tomoya Mizumoto, Mamoru Komachi, Masaaki Nagata, and Yuji Matsumoto. Mining revision log of language learning SNS for automated Japanese error correction of second language learners. In *Proceedings of 5th International Joint Conference on Natural Language Processing*, pages 147–155, Chiang Mai, Thailand, November 2011. Asian Federation of Natural Language Processing. URL http://www.aclweb.org/anthology/I11-1017. 53, 98

Masaki Murata and Makoto Nagao. Determination of referential property and number of nouns in Japanese sentences for machine translation into English. In *Proceedings of the Fifth International Conference on Theoretical and Methodological Issues in Machine Translation*, pages 218–225, Kyoto, Japan, 1993. 105

Kevin P. Murphy. *Machine Learning: A Probabilistic Perspective*. Adaptive computation and machine learning series. MIT Press, 2012. 5

Ryo Nagata and Kazuhide Nakatani. Evaluating performance of grammatical error detection to maximize learning effect. In *Coling 2010: Posters*, pages 894–900, Beijing, China, August 2010. Coling 2010 Organizing Committee. URL http://www.aclweb.org/anthology/C10-2103. 44, 112

Ryo Nagata, Tatsuya Iguchi, Kenta Wakidera, Fumito Masui, and Atsuo Kawai. Recognizing article errors in the writing of Japanese learners of English. *Systems and Computers in Japan*, 36 (7):60–68, 2005a. DOI: 10.1002/scj.20153. 54

Ryo Nagata, Tatsuya Iguchi, Fumito Masui, Atsuo Kawai, and Naoki Isu. A statistical model based on the three head words for detecting article errors. *The Institute of Electronics, Information and Communication Engineers (IEICE) Transactions on Information and Systems*, E88-D(7): 1700–1706, 2005b. DOI: 10.1093/ietisy/e88-d.7.1700. 54

Ryo Nagata, Atsuo Kawai, Koichiro Morihiro, and Naoki Isu. A feedback-augmented method for detecting errors in the writing of learners of English. In *Proceedings of the 21st International Conference of Computational Linguistics (COLING) and 44th Annual Meeting of the Association for Computational Linguistics (ACL)*, pages 241–248, 2006a. DOI: 10.3115/1220175.1220206. 54

Ryo Nagata, Tatsuya Iguchi, Kenta Wakidera, Fumito Masui, Atsuo Kawai, and Naoki Isu. Recognizing article errors using prepositional information. *Systems and Computers in Japan*, 37 (12):873–881, 2006b. DOI: 10.1002/scj.20527. 54

Ryo Nagata, Atsuo Kawai, Koichiro Morihori, and Naoki Isu. Reinforcing English countability prediction with one countability per discourse property. In *Proceedings of the 21st International Conference of Computational Linguistics (COLING) and 44th Annual Meeting of the Association for Computational Linguistics (ACL)*, volume 595–602, 2006c. 54

NCLB. Building partnerships to help english language learners, 2006. URL http://www2.ed .gov/nclb/methods/english/lepfactsheet.pdf. 3

Rani Nelken and Elif Yamangil. Mining Wikipedias article revision history for training computational lingustic algorithms. In *Proceedings of the WIKI-AI: Wikipedia and AI Workshop at the AAAI08 Conference*, Chicago, US, 2008. 97

John Nerbonne. Computer-Assisted Language Learning and Natural Language Processing. In R. Mitkov, editor, *The Oxford Handbook of Computational Linguistics*, pages 670–698. The Oxford University Press, 2003. 4

Nadja Nesselhauf. The use of collocations by advanced learners of English and some implications for teaching. *Applied Linguistics*, 24:223–242, 2003. DOI: 10.1093/applin/24.2.223. 28

Hwee Tou Ng, Siew Mei Wu, Yuanbin Wu, and Joel Tetreault. The CoNLL-2013 shared task on grammatical error correction. In *Proceedings of the Seventeenth Conference on Computational Natural Language Learning*, Sofia, Bulgaria, August 2013. Association for Computational Linguistics. 31, 80, 104

Diane Nicholls. The Cambridge Learner Corpus - error coding and analysis for writing dictionaries and other books for English learners. Presented at the Summer Workshop on Learner Corpora, Showa Woman's University, 1999. 19

Diane Nicholls. Error coding and analysis for lexicography and ELT. In *Proceedings of the Corpus Linguistics 2003 Conference*, pages 572–581, Lancaster, United Kingdom, 2003. 91, 100

Nazlia Omar, Nur Asma Mohd Razali, and Saadiyah Darus. Automated essay marking tool for ESL writing based on heuristics. In *Proceedings of the International Conference of Education, Research and Innovation (ICERI)*, Madrid, 2008. 78

Robert Östling and Ola Knutsson. A corpus-based tool for helping writers with Swedish collocations. In *Proceedings of the Workshop on Extracting and Using Constructions in NLP*, Odense, Denmark, 2009. 72, 78

144 BIBLIOGRAPHY

Y. Albert Park and Roger Levy. Automated whole sentence grammar correction using a noisy channel model. In *Proceedings of the 49th Annual Meeting of the Association for Computational Linguistics: Human Language Technologies*, pages 934–944, Portland, Oregon, USA, June 2011. Association for Computational Linguistics. URL http://www.aclweb.org/anthology/P 11-1094. 107

Pavel Pecina. An extensive empirical study of collocation extraction methods. In *Proceedings of the Student Research Workshop at the 43rd Annual Meeting of the Association for Computational Linguistics (ACL)*, pages 13–18, Ann Arbor, 2005. 66, 69

Ted Pedersen. Fishing for exactness. In *Proceedings of the South-Central SAS Users Group Conference (SCSUG)*, pages 188–200, Austin, TX, 1996. 68

Steven Pinker. *The Language Instinct: The New Science of Language and Mind*. Penguin Books, New York, 1994. 23, 24

David Martin Ward Powers. The problem with kappa. In *Proceedings of the 13th Conference of the European Chapter of the Association for Computational Linguistics*, pages 345–355, Avignon, France, April 2012. Association for Computational Linguistics. URL http://www.aclweb .org/anthology/E12-1035. 33, 34, 35

Desmond Darma Putra and Lili Szabo. UDS at CoNLL 2013 shared task. In *Proceedings of the Seventeenth Conference on Computational Natural Language Learning: Shared Task*, pages 88–95, Sofia, Bulgaria, August 2013. Association for Computational Linguistics. URL http: //www.aclweb.org/anthology/W13-3612.

Li Quan, Oleksandr Kolomiyets, and Marie-Francine Moens. KU Leuven at HOO-2012: A hybrid approach to detection and correction of determiner and preposition errors in non-native English text. In *Proceedings of the Seventh Workshop on Building Educational Applications Using NLP*, pages 263–271, Montréal, Canada, June 2012. Association for Computational Linguistics. URL http://www.aclweb.org/anthology/W12-2031.

Chris Quirk and Arul Menezes. Dependency treelet translation: The convergence of statistical and example-based machine translation? *Machine Translation*, 20(1):43–65, 2006. DOI: 10.1007/s10590-006-9008-4. 10

Randolph Quirk, Sidney Greenbaum, Geoffrey Leech, and Jan Svartvik. *A Comprehensive Grammar of the English Language*. Longman Group, New York, 1985. 26, 27

Margarita Alonso Ramos, Leo Wanner, Orsolya Vincze, Gerard Casamayor del Bosque, Nancy Vázquez Veiga, Estela Mosqueira Suárez, and Sabela Prieto González. Towards a motivated annotation schema of collocation errors in learner corpora. In Nicoletta Calzolari (Conference Chair), Khalid Choukri, Bente Maegaard, Joseph Mariani, Jan Odijk, Stelios

Piperidis, Mike Rosner, and Daniel Tapias, editors, *Proceedings of the Seventh conference on International Language Resources and Evaluation (LREC'10)*, Valletta, Malta, may 2010. European Language Resources Association (ELRA). ISBN 2-9517408-6-7. 66

Yael Ravin. Disambiguating and interpreting verb definitions. In *Proceedings of the 28th Annual Meeting of the Association for Computational Linguistics (ACL)*, pages 260–267, 1990. DOI: 10.3115/981823.981856. 25

Veit Reuer. Error recognition and feedback with Lexical Functional Grammar. *CALICO Journal*, 20(3):497–512, 2003. 7

Stephen Richardson and Lisa Braden-Harder. The experience of developing a large-scale natural language processing system: *Critique*. In *Proceedings of the Second Conference on Applied NLP*, pages 195–202, 1988. DOI: 10.3115/974235.974271. 7

Anne Rimrott and Trude Heift. Language learners and generic spell checkers in CALL. *CALICO*, 23(1):17–48, 2005. 81

Anne Rimrott and Trude Heift. Evaluating automatic detection of misspellings in German. *Language Learning & Technology*, 12(3):73–92, 2008. 81

Alla Rozovskaya and Dan Roth. Annotating ESL errors: Challenges and rewards. In *Proceedings of the HLT-NAACL Fifth Workshop on Building Educational Applications Using NLP*, Los Angeles, 2010a. 91, 92, 120

Alla Rozovskaya and Dan Roth. Generating confusion sets for context-sensitive error correction. In *Proceedings of the 2010 Conference on Empirical Methods in Natural Language Processing*, pages 961–970, Cambridge, MA, October 2010b. Association for Computational Linguistics. URL http://www.aclweb.org/anthology/D10-1094. 52, 101

Alla Rozovskaya and Dan Roth. Training paradigms for correcting errors in grammar and usage. In *Human Language Technologies: The 2010 Annual Conference of the North American Chapter of the Association for Computational Linguistics*, pages 154–162, Los Angeles, California, June 2010c. Association for Computational Linguistics. URL http://www.aclweb.org/anthology/N10-1018. 49, 52, 101

Alla Rozovskaya and Dan Roth. Algorithm selection and model adaptation for ESL correction tasks. In *Proceedings of the 49th Annual Meeting of the Association for Computational Linguistics: Human Language Technologies*, pages 924–933, Portland, Oregon, USA, June 2011. Association for Computational Linguistics. URL http://www.aclweb.org/anthology/P11-1093. 54, 102, 114

Alla Rozovskaya, Mark Sammons, Joshua Gioja, and Dan Roth. University of Illinois system in HOO text correction shared task. In *Proceedings of the Generation Challenges Session at the 13th*

European Workshop on Natural Language Generation, pages 263–266, Nancy, France, September 2011. Association for Computational Linguistics. URL http://www.aclweb.org/antholo gy/W11-2843.

Alla Rozovskaya, Mark Sammons, and Dan Roth. The UI system in the HOO 2012 shared task on error correction. In *Proceedings of the Seventh Workshop on Building Educational Applications Using NLP*, pages 272–280, Montréal, Canada, June 2012. Association for Computational Linguistics. URL http://www.aclweb.org/anthology/W12-2032. 100, 102

Alla Rozovskaya, Kai-Wei Chang, Mark Sammons, and Dan Roth. The University of Illinois system in the CoNLL-2013 shared task. In *Proceedings of the Seventeenth Conference on Computational Natural Language Learning: Shared Task*, pages 13–19, Sofia, Bulgaria, August 2013. Association for Computational Linguistics. URL http://www.aclweb.org/anthology/W13-3602. 80, 104

Keisuke Sakaguchi, Yuta Hayashibe, Shuhei Kondo, Lis Kanashiro, Tomoya Mizumoto, Mamoru Komachi, and Yuji Matsumoto. NAIST at the HOO 2012 shared task. In *Proceedings of the Seventh Workshop on Building Educational Applications Using NLP*, pages 281–288, Montréal, Canada, June 2012a. Association for Computational Linguistics. URL http://www.aclweb.org/anthology/W12-2033.

Keisuke Sakaguchi, Tomoya Mizumoto, Mamoru Komachi, and Yuji Matsumoto. Joint English speling error correction and POS tagging for language learners writing. In *Proceedings of the 12th International Conference on Computational Linguistics (COLING)*, pages 2357–2374, 2012b. 82

David Schneider and Kathleen McCoy. Recognizing syntactic errors in the writing of second language learners. In *Proceedings of the 36th Annual Meeting of the Association for Computational Linguistics (ACL) and the 17th International Conference on Computational Linguistics (COLING)*, pages 1198–1204, Montreal, 1998. DOI: 10.3115/980691.980765. 8

Ethel Schuster. The role of native grammars in correcting errors in second language learning. *Computational Intelligence*, 2:93–98, 1986. DOI: 10.1111/j.1467-8640.1986.tb00074.x. 9

Camilla B. Schwind. Sensitive parsing: Error analysis and explanation in an intelligent language tutoring system. In *Proceedings of the Twelfth International Conference on Computational Linguistics (COLING)*, pages 608–618, 1988. 9

Camilla B. Schwind. Feature grammars for semantic analysis. *Computer Intelligence*, 6:172–178, 1990a. DOI: 10.1111/j.1467-8640.1990.tb00132.x. 8

Camilla B. Schwind. An intelligent language tutoring system. *Journal of Man-Mchine Studies*, 33:557–579, 1990b. 9

Camilla B. Schwind. Error analysis and explanation in knowledge language tutoring. *Computer Assisted Language Learning*, 8(4):295–324, 1995. DOI: 10.1080/0958822950080402. 8

Younghee Sheen. The effect of focused written corrective feedback and language aptitude on ESL learners' acquisition of articles. *TESOL Quarterly*, 41:255–283, 2007. DOI: 10.1002/j.1545-7249.2007.tb00059.x. 110

Chi-Chiang Shei and Helen Pain. An ESL writer's collocational aid. *Computer Assisted Language Learning*, 13(2):167–182, 2000. DOI: 10.1076/0958-8221(200004)13:2;1-D;FT167. 72

Victor Sheng, Foster Provost, and Panagiotis Ipeirotis. Get another label? Improving data quality and data mining using multiple, noisy labelers. In *Proceeding of the ACM Special Interest Group on Knowledge Discovery and Data Mining (ACM-SIGKDD)*, Las Vegas, Nevada, 2008. DOI: 10.1145/1401890.1401965. 95

Sayori Shimohata, Toshiyuki Sugio, and Junji Nagata. Retrieving collocations by co-occurrences and word order constraints. In *Proceedings of the Eighth Conference of the European Chapter of the Association for Computational Linguistics (EACL)*, pages 476–481, Madrid, 1997. DOI: 10.3115/979617.979678. 66

Grigori Sidorov, Anubhav Gupta, Martin Tozer, Dolors Catala, Angels Catena, and Sandrine Fuentes. Rule-based system for automatic grammar correction using syntactic *n*-grams for English language learning (L2). In *Proceedings of the Seventeenth Conference on Computational Natural Language Learning: Shared Task*, pages 96–101, Sofia, Bulgaria, August 2013. Association for Computational Linguistics. URL http://www.aclweb.org/anthology/W13-3613.

Jonas Sjöbergh and Ola Knutsson. Faking errors to avoid making errors: Very weakly supervised learning for error detection in writing. In *Proceedings of the International Conference on Recent Advances in Natural Language Processing (RANLP)*, pages 506–512, Borovets, Bulgaria, 2005. 51

D. Sleeman. Mis-generalisation: An explanation of observed mal-rules. In *Proceedings of the Sixth Annual Conference of the Cognitive Science Society*, pages 51–56, 1984. 8

Rion Snow, Brendan O'Connor, Daniel Jurafsky, and Andrew Ng. Cheap and fast – but is it good? Evaluating non-expert annotations for natural language tasks. In *Proceedings of the 2008 Conference on Empirical Methods in Natural Language Processing (EMNLP)*, pages 254–263, Honolulu, Hawaii, 2008. DOI: 10.3115/1613715.1613751. 95, 97

Guihua Sun, Xiaohua Liu, Gao Cong, Ming Zhou, Zhongyang Xiong, John Lee, and Chin-Yew Lin. Detecting erroneous sentences using automatically mined sequential patterns. In *Proceedings of the 45th Annual Meeting of the Association for Computational Linguistics*, pages 81–88, 2007. 83

Patrick Suppes, Dan Flickinger, Elizabeth Macken, Jeanette Cook, and Tie Liang. Description of the epgy stanford university online courses for mathematics and the language arts. In *Proceedings of the International Society for Technology in Education*, San Diego, CA, USA, June 2012. 8

Michael Swan and Bernard Smith, editors. *Learner English: A teacher's guide to interference and other problems.* Cambridge University Press, 2 edition, 2001. DOI: 10.1017/CBO9780511667121. 21, 25

Toshikazu Tajiri, Mamoru Komachi, and Yuji Matsumoto. Tense and aspect error correction for ESL learners using global context. In *Proceedings of the 50th Annual Meeting of the Association for Computational Linguistics (Volume 2: Short Papers)*, pages 198–202, Jeju Island, Korea, July 2012. Association for Computational Linguistics. URL http://www.aclweb.org/anthology/P12-2039. 53, 79, 80, 98

Joel Tetreault and Martin Chodorow. The ups and downs of preposition error detection in ESL writing. In *Proceedings of the 22nd International Conference on Computational Linguistics (COLING)*, pages 865–872, 2008a. 31, 50, 55, 57

Joel Tetreault and Martin Chodorow. Native Judgments of non-native usage: Experiments in preposition error detection. In *Proceedings of the Workshop on Human Judgments in Computational Linguistics at the 22nd International Conference on Computational Linguistics (COLING)*, pages 24–32, 2008b. 37, 39, 40, 41, 87, 91, 92, 93, 94

Joel Tetreault and Martin Chodorow. Examining the use of region web counts for ESL error detection. In *Proceedings of the Web as Corpus Workshop (WAC-5)*, San Sebastian, Spain, 2009. 55, 57, 58, 59, 114

Joel Tetreault, Elena Filatova, and Martin Chodorow. Rethinking grammatical error annotation and evaluation with the Amazon Mechanical Turk. In *Proceedings of the NAACL HLT 2010 Fifth Workshop on Innovative Use of NLP for Building Educational Applications*, pages 45–48, Los Angeles, California, June 2010a. Association for Computational Linguistics. URL http://www.aclweb.org/anthology/W10-1006. 42, 95, 96

Joel Tetreault, Jennifer Foster, and Martin Chodorow. Using parse features for preposition selection and error detection. In *Proceedings of the ACL 2010 Conference Short Papers*, pages 353–358, Uppsala, Sweden, July 2010b. Association for Computational Linguistics. URL http://www.aclweb.org/anthology/P10-2065. 55

Joel Tetreault, Daniel Blanchard, Aoife Cahill, and Martin Chodorow. Native tongues, lost and found: Resources and empirical evaluations in native language identification. In *Proceedings of COLING 2012*, pages 2585–2602, Mumbai, India, December 2012. The COLING 2012 Organizing Committee. URL http://www.aclweb.org/anthology/C12-1158. 114

Joel Tetreault, Martin Chodorow, and Nitin Madnani. Bucking the trend: improved evaluation and annotation practices for ESL error detection systems. *Language Resources and Evaluation*, pages 1–27, 2013. ISSN 1574-020X. DOI: 10.1007/s10579-013-9243-2. 95

John Truscott. The case against grammar correction in L2 writing classes. *Language Learning*, 46:327–369, 1996. DOI: 10.1111/j.1467-1770.1996.tb01238.x. 109

Jenine Turner and Eugene Charniak. Language modeling for determiner selection. In *Proceedings of Human Language Technologies: The Annual Conference of the North American Chapter of the Association for Computational Linguistics, Companion Volume*, pages 177–180, Rochester, NY, 2007. 56

Larraitz Uria, Bertol Arrieta, Arantza Díaz de Ilarraza, Montse Maritxalar, and Maite Oronoz. Determiner errors in Basque: Analysis and automatic detection. *Procesamiento del Lenguaje Natural*, pages 41–48, 2009. 78

Antal van den Bosch and Peter Berck. Memory-based text correction for preposition and determiner errors. In *Proceedings of the Seventh Workshop on Building Educational Applications Using NLP*, pages 289–294, Montréal, Canada, June 2012. Association for Computational Linguistics. URL http://www.aclweb.org/anthology/W12-2034.

Antal van den Bosch and Peter Berck. Memory-based grammatical error correction. In *Proceedings of the Seventeenth Conference on Computational Natural Language Learning: Shared Task*, pages 102–108, Sofia, Bulgaria, August 2013. Association for Computational Linguistics. URL http://www.aclweb.org/anthology/W13-3614.

Carl Vogel and Robin Cooper. Robust chart parsing with mildly inconsistent feature structures. In A. Schöter and C. Vogel, editors, *Nonclassical Feature Systems*, pages 197–216. Centre for Cognitive Science, University of Edinburgh, Working Papers in Cognitive Science, 1995. Volume 10. 8

Joachim Wagner. *Detection grammatical errors with treebank-induced, probabilistic parsers.* PhD thesis, Dublin City University, Dublin, Ireland, 2012. 35

Joachim Wagner, Jennifer Foster, and Josef van Genabith. A comparative evaluation of deep and shallow approaches to the automatic detection of common grammatical errors. In *Proceedings of the Joint Conference on Empirical Methods in Natural Language Processing and Computational Natural Language Learning (EMNLP and CONLL)*, pages 112–121, 2007. 51

Joachim Wagner, Jennifer Foster, and Josef van Genabith. Judging grammaticality: Experiments in sentence classification. *CALICO Journal*, 26(3):474–490, 2009. 51

Ralph Weischedel, Wilfried M. Voge, and Mark James. An artificial intelligence approach to language instruction. *Artificial Intelligence*, 10:225–240, 1978. DOI: 10.1016/S0004-3702(78)80015-0. 9

Randy West, Y. Albert Park, and Roger Levy. Bilingual random walk models for automated grammar correction of ESL author-produced text. In *Proceedings of the Sixth Workshop on Innovative Use of NLP for Building Educational Applications*, pages 170–179, Portland, Oregon, June 2011. Association for Computational Linguistics. URL http://www.aclweb.org/anthology/W11-1421. 107

Casey Whitelaw, Ben Hutchinson, Grace Y. Chung, and Ged Ellis. Using the Web for language independent spellchecking and autocorrection. In *Proceedings of the Conference on Empirical Methods in Natural Language Processing (EMNLP)*, pages 890–899, Singapore, 2009. 81

David Wible, Chin-Hwa Kwo, Nai-Lung Tsao, Anne Liu, and Hsiu-Ling Lin. Bootstrapping in a language learning environment. *Journal of Computer Assisted Learning*, 19(4):90–102, 2003. DOI: 10.1046/j.0266-4909.2002.00009.x. 28, 72

David Wible, Chin-Hwa Kuo, Meng-Chang Chen, Nai-Lung Tsao, and Tsung-Fu Hung. A computational approach to the discovery and representation of lexical chunks. In *Proceedings of the 13th Conference Sur Le Traitement Automatique des Langues Naturelles (TALN)*, pages 868–875, Leuven, 2006. 71

L. Amber Wilcox-O'Hearn. A noisy channel model framework for grammatical correction. In *Proceedings of the Seventeenth Conference on Computational Natural Language Learning: Shared Task*, pages 109–114, Sofia, Bulgaria, August 2013. Association for Computational Linguistics. URL http://www.aclweb.org/anthology/W13-3615.

Alison Wray. Formulaic sequences in second language teaching. *Applied Linguistics*, 21(4), 2000. DOI: 10.1093/applin/21.4.463. 27

Jian-Cheng Wu, Yu-Chia Chang, Teruko Mitamura, and Jason S. Chang. Automatic collocation suggestion in academic writing. In *Proceedings of the ACL 2010 Conference Short Papers*, pages 115–119, Uppsala, Sweden, July 2010. Association for Computational Linguistics. URL http://www.aclweb.org/anthology/P10-2021. 73

Jian-Cheng Wu, Joseph Chang, Yi-Chun Chen, Shih-Ting Huang, Mei-Hua Chen, and Jason S. Chang. Helping Our Own: NTHU NLPLAB system description. In *Proceedings of the Seventh Workshop on Building Educational Applications Using NLP*, pages 295–301, Montréal, Canada, June 2012. Association for Computational Linguistics. URL http://www.aclweb.org/anthology/W12-2035.

Yang Xiang, Bo Yuan, Yaoyun Zhang, Xiaolong Wang, Wen Zheng, and Chongqiang Wei. A hybrid model for grammatical error correction. In *Proceedings of the Seventeenth Conference on Computational Natural Language Learning: Shared Task*, pages 115–122, Sofia, Bulgaria, August 2013. Association for Computational Linguistics. URL http://www.aclweb.org/anthology/W13-3616.

Junwen Xing, Longyue Wang, Derek F. Wong, Lidia S. Chao, and Xiaodong Zeng. Um-checker: A hybrid system for English grammatical error correction. In *Proceedings of the Seventeenth Conference on Computational Natural Language Learning: Shared Task*, pages 34–42, Sofia, Bulgaria, August 2013. Association for Computational Linguistics. URL http://www.aclweb.org/anthology/W13-3605. 80

Helen Yannakoudakis, Ted Briscoe, and Ben Medlock. A new dataset and method for automatically grading ESOL texts. In *Proceedings of the 49th Annual Meeting of the Association for Computational Linguistics: Human Language Technologies*, pages 180–189, Portland, Oregon, USA, June 2011. Association for Computational Linguistics. URL http://www.aclweb.org/anthology/P11-1019. 98, 101

David Yarowsky. Decision lists for lexical ambiguity resolution: Application to accent restoration in Spanish and French. In *Proceedings of the 32nd Annual Meeting of the Association for Computational Linguistics (ACL)*, pages 88–95, Las Cruces, NM, 1994. DOI: 10.3115/981732.981745. 13

Bong-Jun Yi, Ho-Chang Lee, and Hae-Chang Rim. Kunlp grammatical error correction system for CoNLL-2013 shared task. In *Proceedings of the Seventeenth Conference on Computational Natural Language Learning: Shared Task*, pages 123–127, Sofia, Bulgaria, August 2013. Association for Computational Linguistics. URL http://www.aclweb.org/anthology/W13-3617.

Xing Yi, Jianfeng Gao, and William B. Dolan. A web-based English proofing system for English as a second language users. In *Proceedings of the International Joint Conference on Natural Language Processing (IJCNLP)*, pages 619–624, Hyderabad, India, 2008. 57, 58

Ippei Yoshimoto, Tomoya Kose, Kensuke Mitsuzawa, Keisuke Sakaguchi, Tomoya Mizumoto, Yuta Hayashibe, Mamoru Komachi, and Yuji Matsumoto. NAIST at 2013 CoNLL grammatical error correction shared task. In *Proceedings of the Seventeenth Conference on Computational Natural Language Learning: Shared Task*, pages 26–33, Sofia, Bulgaria, August 2013. Association for Computational Linguistics. URL http://www.aclweb.org/anthology/W13-3604.

Zheng Yuan and Mariano Felice. Constrained grammatical error correction using statistical machine translation. In *Proceedings of the Seventeenth Conference on Computational Natural Language Learning: Shared Task*, pages 52–61, Sofia, Bulgaria, August 2013. Association for Computational Linguistics. URL http://www.aclweb.org/anthology/W13-3607.

Torsten Zesch. Helping Our Own 2011: UKP lab system description. In *Proceedings of the Generation Challenges Session at the 13th European Workshop on Natural Language Generation*, pages 260–262, Nancy, France, September 2011. Association for Computational Linguistics. URL http://www.aclweb.org/anthology/W11-2842. 80

Torsten Zesch. Measuring contextual fitness using error contexts extracted from the Wikipedia revision history. In *Proceedings of the 13th Conference of the European Chapter of the Association for Computational Linguistics*, pages 529–538, Avignon, France, April 2012. Association for Computational Linguistics. URL http://www.aclweb.org/anthology/E12-1054. 97

Torsten Zesch and Jens Haase. HOO 2012 shared task: UKP Lab system description. In *Proceedings of the Seventh Workshop on Building Educational Applications Using NLP*, pages 302–306, Montréal, Canada, June 2012. Association for Computational Linguistics. URL http://www.aclweb.org/anthology/W12-2036.

Alan X. Zhang. *English collocations and their effect on the writing of native and non-native College Freshmen*. PhD thesis, Indiana University of Pennsylvania, Pennsylvania, 1993. 27

Authors' Biographies

CLAUDIA LEACOCK

Claudia Leacock is a Research Scientist III at CTB McGraw-Hill where she works on methods for automated scoring. Previously, as a consultant with the Butler Hill Group, she collaborated with the Microsoft Research team that developed *ESL Assistant*, a web-based prototype tool for detecting and correcting grammatical errors of English language learners. As a Distinguished Member of Technical Staff at Pearson Knowledge Technologies (2004–2007), and previously as a Principal Development Scientist at Educational Testing Service (1997–2004), she developed tools for both automated assessment of short-answer content-based questions and grammatical error detection and correction. As a member of the WordNet group at Princeton University's Cognitive Science Lab (1991–1997), her research focused on word sense disambiguation. Dr. Leacock received a B.A. in English from NYU, a Ph.D. in linguistics from the City University of New York, Graduate Center, and was a post-doctoral fellow at IBM, T.J. Watson Research Center.

MARTIN CHODOROW

Martin Chodorow received his Ph.D. in cognitive psychology (psycholinguistics) from MIT. Following a two-year postdoctoral position in computational linguistics at IBM's Thomas Watson Research Center, he joined the faculty of Hunter College and the Graduate School of the City University of New York, where he is Professor of Psychology & Linguistics. His NLP research interests include measurement of text similarity and automated assessment of writing. He has served as a consultant for IBM, Princeton University's Cognitive Science Laboratory, and, for the past 16 years, Educational Testing Service, where he works on the grammatical error detection system in ETS's e-rater essay scoring engine and *Criterion Online Writing Service*. His current research in cognitive psychology examines the psychological processes that underlie proofreading.

MICHAEL GAMON

Michael Gamon is a researcher in the Natural Language Processing Group at Microsoft Research. He joined Microsoft Research after receiving his Ph.D. in linguistics from the University of Washington in 1996. He worked first on developing the German computational grammar which is used in the *Word* grammar checker and became interested in the specific problems of language learners at that time. Subsequently he has done research in a number of areas, from natural language generation to sentiment detection, language in social media, and query classification. In the past several years he has been working on the Microsoft Research *ESL Assistant* (www.eslassistant.com), a prototype web service for detection and correction of grammatical errors of English language learners. His current interests include more flexible data-driven algorithms for grammatical error detection.

JOEL TETREAULT

Joel Tetreault is Senior Research Scientist at Yahoo! Labs in New York City. His research focus is Natural Language Processing with specific interests in anaphora, dialogue and discourse processing, machine learning, and applying these techniques to the analysis of English language learning and automated essay scoring. Previously he was Principal Manager of the Core Natural Language group at Nuance Communications, Inc., where he worked on the research and development of NLP tools and components for the next generation of intelligent dialogue systems. Prior to Nuance, he worked at Educational Testing Service for six years as a managing research scientist where he researched automated methods for detecting grammatical errors by non-native speakers, plagiarism detection, and content scoring. Tetreault received his B.A. in Computer Science from Harvard University (1998) and his M.S. and Ph.D. in Computer Science from the University of Rochester (2004). He was also a postdoctoral research scientist at the University of Pittsburgh's Learning Research and Development Center (2004–2007), where he worked on developing spoken dialogue tutoring systems.